Copyright Catechism

Practical Answers to Everyday School Dilemmas

Carol Simpson

Professional Development Resources for
K-12 Library Media and Technology Specialists

Library of Congress Cataloging-in-Publication Data

Simpson, Carol, 1949-
  Copyright catechism : practical answers to everyday school dilemmas / Carol Simpson.
     p. cm.
   ISBN 1-58683-202-6 (pbk.)
  1. Copyright--United States. 2. Copyright--United States--Miscellanea. 3. Fair use (Copyright)--United States. 4. Fair use (Copyright)--United States--Miscellanea. I. Simpson, Carol, 1949- Copyright for schools 4th ed. II. Title.
KF2995.S56 2005
346.7304'82--dc22
                                2005018524

Cyndee Anderson: Acquisitions Editor
Carol Simpson: Editorial Director
Judi Repman: Consulting Editor

Published by Linworth Publishing, Inc.
480 East Wilson Bridge Road, Suite L
Worthington, Ohio 43085

Copyright © 2005 by Linworth Publishing, Inc.

All rights reserved. Reproduction of this book in whole or in parts is prohibited without permission of the publisher.

ISBN: 1-58683-202-6

5 4 3 2 1

Table of Contents

About the Author viii
Introduction ix

Chapter One: Ownership of Copyright 1
   Generally 3
      Copyright in MARC Records .3
      Copyright vs. Trademark 4
      Downloading MARC Records 5
      Guidelines vs. Fair Use Analysis 6
      Innocent Infringers 7
      International Copyright 8
      Sharing MARC Records 9
   Protected or Not? 10
      Copyrighting Your Work 10
      Document Protection 11
   Student Work 12
      Displaying Student Work 12
      Online Worksheets 13
   Work for Hire 14
      Copyright of Q and A 14
      Copyright of Teacher Made Materials 15
      School Organization Logo .16
      Web Page Ownership 17
      Work Hired by School 18

Chapter Two: Print Materials 19
   Fair Use 20
      Audio Copies of Books 20
      Audio Recording of Book Chapters 21
      Audio Recording of Books .22
      Comic Superheroes 23
      Copies of Song Lyrics 24
      Copying Educational Periodicals 25
      Copying to Substitute for Textbooks 26
      Copying Workbooks 27
      Copyright Clearance Center Charges 28
      Copyright of Famous Speeches 29
      Fair Use vs. License 30
      Fill-in-the-Blank Textbooks .31
      Folktales 32
      ILL Copying 33

        Is the Bible Public Domain? .34
        Kurzweil Scanners 35
        Legal Sources of Reading Passages 36
        Lending a Bound Periodical .37
        Movie Scripts Online 38
        Nine Instances of Multiple Copying 39
        Out-of-Print Book Copies 40
        Photocopies of Internet Pages 41
        Poster Making 42
        Presenting Student Work at a Conference 43
        Proof of Sources 44
        Publishing Student Work 45
        Recording Books on Audiotape 46
        Recording Books on Tape 47
        Recording Picture Books 48
        Reproducible Magazines 49
        Rule of Five 50
        Student Cookbook 51
        Student-Made Anthologies 52
        Taping Books for Special Education 53
        Vertical Files 54
        Worksheets on the Web 55
  Public Display 56
        Puppet Show Adaptations 56

Chapter Three: Graphic Materials 57
  Fair Use 59
        Art Masterpiece Museum Brochure 59
        Citing Book Covers 60
        Clip Art 61
        Cover Art on the Web 62
        Creating a Derivative Work .63
        Displaying Book Covers 64
        Fair Use and Pictures on the Web 65
        Images of Public Art 66
        Making Copies of Images 67
        Newspaper Pictures 68
        PowerPoint Picture Books 69
        Reproducing Images in Newsletters 70
        Web Page Images 71
        Web Pictures 72
  Public Display 73
        Book Character Murals 73
        Cartoon Images 74

      Displaying Book Covers on the Web 75
      Displaying Cartoons 76
      Graphics and Music Manuscripts 77
      Graphics Over Channel One 78
      Home Use Only Video 79
      Photocopy Pictures for Bulletin Boards 80
      Photographs of Paintings 81
      Student Copies Church Painting 82
      Taking Graphics from the Internet 83
      Using Book Characters for Murals 84

Chapter Four: Sound Recordings and Music 85
    Generally 88
      Archival Copies of Audiotapes 88
      Archiving Books on CD 89
      Band Music 90
      Citing Music Sources 91
      Fair Use of Downloaded Music 92
      Mechanical Reproduction Rights of Musicals 93
      Online Music for Video 94
      Replacing Damaged Audio Recording 95
      Selling Copies of Videotaped Music Performance . . .96
      Using a Song on CCT 97
    In Class 98
      Helping Students with Low Reading Ability 98
      Making Band Music Available via Password 99
      Music in Student Productions 100
      Music Performance 101
      Public Domain Songs 102
    Public Performance 103
      Audio CDs for Workshops 103
      Broadcasting a Musical Program 104
      Broadcasting School Music 105
      Choir Caroling 106
      Downloaded Music 107
      Internet Radio 108
      Music in Multimedia 109
      Music Recording Performance 110
      Playing Classical Music for Inspiration 111
      Songs During Graduation 112
      Using Background Music 113

Chapter Five: Video and Film 115
   Generally 117
      Archival Copies of Video 117
      AV Restrictions 118
      Copies for Kids 119
      Download Data from Disc to Video 120
      Editing Questionable Videos 121
      Film Collection for Students 122
      Loaning Videos 123
      Mail Order Video Expurgation 124
      No-Library-Loan Video 125
      Off-Air Taping 126
      Parent Videotaping Musical Performance 127
      PBS Tape Retention 128
      Spontaneity and Providing Lists to Teachers 129
      Using Video Distribution Systems 130
      Video Anthology 131
      Video Edited for Content 132
      Video Licensing 133
   In Class 134
      After School Movie Showings 134
      Making a Videotape Anthology 135
      Peripheral Movie Showings 136
      Private Home Exhibition Label 137
      Public Domain Video or Not? 138
      Rainy-Day Video Situations 139
      Satellite Television 140
      Showing a Movie for a Grade-Wide Unit 141
      Showing Movie Clips 142
      Spanish Cable 143
      Special Education Video Reward 144
      Student Provides Video for Educational Purposes ... 145
      Taping Off Cable 146
      Teacher Owned Disney Films 147
      Videotaped Booktalks 148
   Public Performance 149
      Broadcasting a Video 149
      Charging Movie Admission Fees 150
      Licensing for DVDs and Videos 151
      Number of Program Showings Allowed 152
      Private Showings in Movie Theaters 153
      Showing Movies on Busses 154
      Showing Videos to the Entire School 155

Synch Rights with Video 156
Taping Episodes of a PBS Series 157
Video PPR 158

Chapter Six: Multimedia, Software, and Distance Learning .159
  Generally 161
    AR AWOL 161
    Burning CDs 162
    Discontinued Software 163
    Donated Software 164
    Fair Use on the Web? 165
    Installing Computer Software 166
    Installing Single-User CDs 167
    Installing Software on Circulating Computers 168
    Lab Pack License 169
    Linking Internet Sites 170
    Linking Web Sites 171
    Partial CD Installation Permission 172
    URL Bookmarks 173
  Multimedia 174
    Background Music 174
    Borrowing Theme Music from Video 175
    Electronic Portfolio and Copyright Permissions 176
    Looping 177
    Movie Clips in PowerPoint 178
    Scanning Worksheets 179
    Showing Student-Made Multimedia Products 180
    Student Multimedia in Staff Development 181
    Using Music in PowerPoint 182
    Workshop Use of a Student Multimedia Project 183
  Distance Learning 184
    Rules for Video Use in Distance Learning 184

Chapter Seven: Management of Copyright 185
  Policies 186
    Copyright Policy 186
    Finding a Copyright Attorney 187
  Documentation 188
    Photocopier Warning Notice 188
    Site License Definition 189

Chapter Eight: Permissions Issues 191
    Central Reproduction 192
    Publisher Permission 192

Table of Contents **vii**

Introduction

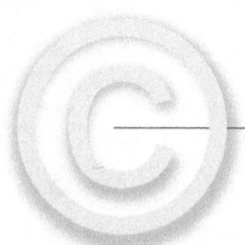

This book is intended as a companion to *Copyright for Schools: A Practical Guide, 4th Edition* (Linworth Publishing, Inc., 2005). While not containing the detail to be a primary resource on copyright, this book includes 177 questions taken from *Technology Connection*, *The Book Report*, *Library Talk*, and *Library Media Connection*, plus new questions not yet published. All questions have been updated to reflect the state of law as of summer 2005. All questions were initially submitted by educators, and genericized for broadest application. All situations are based on activities in K-12 public/non-profit schools, though many will apply in pre-school, religious school, community organization, day care center, college and university applications. Before making assumptions about applicability, however, consult an attorney to verify that the same conditions apply.

The most common use for the questions here is to present practical application of copyright practice to educators who may not know or accept it. In fact, the questions and answers may be used to convince reluctant educators that their erroneous assumptions about common educational practices are incorrect. It's important to recognize that these questions are not legal advice. The author is not an attorney, and recommends that complex copyright problems be discussed with a school district's retained counsel or an attorney who specializes in intellectual property. Each situation is unique, and certain combinations of facts may yield a totally different outcome than the examples here. Use the questions as a starting point for discussion and consideration, not as an unequivocal answer.

Remember as you read the questions, keep in mind that it is essential to assert all available fair use rights, lest they be deemed to be extraneous. Free use of limited amounts of copyright protected materials for the purpose of educating students is part of copyright law. However, courts are more and more likely to find that licensing is a viable alternative to fair use. If educators hope to retain this limited right, they must be prepared to invoke the right on every available occasion, without apologies. Publishers must also be prepared to concede the small bits of material that are available for use on a limited basis. In return, educators need to follow the rules so that publishers make enough money to continue to publish the materials the educators find so attractive. It's only fair.

C.S.

Chapter One

Ownership of Copyright

Copyright in the United States is not something you must request, register, or record. Copyright just happens. The moment something is put into "tangible form," the creator of the work owns a copyright in that work. The creator does not need to do anything special to gain a copyright. No notice is required; no registration forms or fees are needed. The copyright affixes to the work the moment it is written on paper, saved to disk, painted on canvas, recorded on tape, or exposed onto film. The once ubiquitous c-in-a-circle mark may be present or absent. The creator owns all the six rights of a copyright owner at that point.

The term "creator" is significant. A work must have a modicum of creativity to be eligible for copyright protection. Facts are not protectable by copyright. Works that have enjoyed a full term of copyright protection can no longer be protected by copyright, even if they are reproduced in a new edition. However, if someone were to create an adaptation of such a work (also called a work in the public domain), or provide added content to a public domain work (such as new illustrations to *Oliver Twist*), the new additions would be protected for the full term of copyright protection, while the original parts would not.

The current duration of copyright is the life of the author (or the longest lived author, if there are more than one) plus 70 years. In the case of a corporate author (such as a motion picture, where no one person can be identified as the author of the work), the duration of copyright is for 95 years from the date of creation.

During the time of protection, copyrights may be bought, sold, rented, leased, and transferred just as other property. Transfer of copyright must be in writing. While one must be of the age of majority to sign documents relating to transfers of property, including copyrights, one need not be of any particular age to create a work that is protected by copyright. As you will see in the questions below, many of these straightforward facts affect the use of copyrighted materials within schools.

Generally | Copyright in MARC Records

? *Several online library catalogs include downloadable Machine-Readable Cataloging (MARC) on their materials. Is it copyright infringement if we use the downloaded MARC record for our catalog?*

© Many MARC records emanate from the Library of Congress (LOC). Because LOC is a U.S. government entity, nothing from them can be copyrighted. So, there are no problems using LOC records or records that initially came from LOC because they are in the public domain. Since cataloging is mostly a transcription of facts from the item being cataloged, that portion of the record cannot be protected either. (Facts cannot be protected by copyright, only the creative expression of those facts.) About the only part of the record that might be considered creative would be the summary, and that is a minimal part of the record.

All that being said, I will say that the Online Computer Library Center (OCLC) claims copyright on their records, and attempts to defend that position. I'm not sure how successful they have been in protecting that claim.

Generally | Copyright vs. Trademark

? *A student designed a logo that he wants to have embroidered on team shirts. Someone who saw his design told him that it is already in use, and is copyrighted (trademarked?) How do we find out if "his" design is already protected by copyright? Is there a database to search, and how would you search for a design, anyway? Does he send his design to some government office (address?) and ask to have it trademarked, and let them tell him it's already used? How do I help him?*

© Trademarks must be in use in a particular industry (Apple is a trademark in computers and in recordings, for example), and it is the design that is specific, not just the words used (though they can be trademarked, as well). The point of trademark is to avoid confusion among companies and brands, and to minimize misrepresentations. When a design is similar to one in use in another area, the original trademark owner can claim "dilution of a trademark."

The trademark office maintains the registrations, but most folks must hire someone to search the files. Some are online, but only when there is a searchable word or letter combination. However, it is possible to violate the trademark of an UNregistered mark, as well as a registered one (just like copyrights), so a search is advisable. When doing the search be sure to search for similar marks, like alligator and crocodile, or zephyr and cipher. Those can infringe in certain circumstances.

Generally | Downloading MARC Records

? *Is downloading MARC records for use in our catalog a violation of copyright? If I use the same information in a publication, is it a violation? I want to use the summary statement from the MARC records in a published list and want to be sure that I am not violating copyright. Also, if we publish our catalog on the Web, we are distributing the information, so is this a violation?*

© The answer to your question depends on where your records come from. Records created by the Library of Congress are public domain by law. Federal employees in the course of their jobs create them, so they have no copyright. OCLC, however, does claim copyright on records in their database. Some school districts and consortia also claim copyright on MARC records. If you get your records from a vendor, you might want to know where the records came from before you make extensive use of the summaries. The author and title information are facts and as such are likely not protected. But the summary is a bit more creative, so there could be a claim of copyright on that information.

Generally | Guidelines vs. Fair Use Analysis

? *It was my understanding that the fair use guidelines outlined exactly what and how much can be copied. Yet, I read an article stating that although these guidelines are part of legislative history and have been referred to in court cases, they are not law. If these specific guidelines are not law, then how can teachers be held liable if they use copyrighted materials in excess of the stated amounts? It seems to me that if the teacher believes they have fulfilled the four criteria for fair use, then copying, for example, 1,200 words instead of 1,000 words should be acceptable. It seems to me that the four factors are more lenient regarding educational use than the guidelines.*

© The various guidelines are not law, however they have the force of law. They have been read into the Congressional Record and "blessed," as it were, so that courts must consider those guidelines as being the intent of Congress. The Guidelines are baselines from which to proceed, not hard and fast upper limits. They are a safe harbor. You KNOW that if you follow the guidelines you will be okay. But one may always perform a fair use analysis based on the four factors and if you come up with a positive result you may wish to risk the usage beyond the fair use guideline limits. The four factors are very subjective whereas the guidelines are very easy to follow. There is little argument over 1,000 words, but there is a MAJOR argument (hence legal fees, court costs, etc.) if someone decided to challenge that your use has an effect on the market for a given work, for example. I generally recommend folks look first at the guidelines. If those limits absolutely cannot meet the need, a fair use analysis is in order. If your objective fair use analysis is marginal, either consult a copyright attorney for a legal opinion, or plan to license your use of that work.

Generally | Innocent Infringers

? *The Digital Millennium Copyright Act has a special exemption for schools and libraries called "innocent infringers." Does that mean schools no longer have to worry about copyright suits?*

© No. The text of the law says, "(B) NONPROFIT LIBRARY, ARCHIVES, OR EDUCATIONAL INSTITUTIONS—In the case of a nonprofit library, archives, or educational institution, the court shall remit damages in any case in which the library, archives, or educational institution sustains the burden of proving, and the court finds, that the library, archives, or educational institution was not aware and had no reason to believe that its acts constituted a violation." The point to remember is that ignorance of the law is not a defense. As citizens we are obligated to know and understand the law. This exception is for cases in which you honestly felt you were within the letter of the law, and the court concurs.

Chapter One: Ownership of Copyright

Generally | International Copyright

? *Could you give me a simplified version of just what the international copyright law says? I teach in a school overseas, and I'm not sure what the rules are.*

© There is no such thing as "international" copyright law. Each country has its own laws. If the country in which you teach is a signatory to the Berne Convention, they protect the intellectual property of other countries under their own laws. You need to find out what your country's copyright law is, and if they signed Berne. Then you will know where you stand.

Generally | Sharing MARC Records

? *Can we share MARC records? I thought that if they were purchased from a company, such as Marcive, Inc. or provided by a vendor, they may not be copied. Is this correct?*

© It will depend on your contract with that vendor. Some vendors use many records from the Library of Congress (LOC). Works of the LOC are in the public domain by law. However, if a private organization (such as OCLC) created the record, it is possible they might contend to own a copyright on the record. That assertion is suspect because facts (e.g., the title transcribed from the title page) are not protectable. About the only part of the record one might be able to claim a copyright on would be the summary.

Protected or Not? | Copyrighting Your Work

? *If a person has written something that will be used as an internal document, and wants to be sure to be credited as the creator of it, is it enough to write "copyright so-and-so 2005" on the cover? If not, what is the procedure?*

© No notice of copyright is needed, but there are other questions to ask. Was this document written as part of someone's employment (which this sounds like)? If so, the copyright in the document is owned by the employer, not the employee. Does the author intend to sue if the copyright (assuming it is the author's and not the employer's) is infringed? If so, the document must be REGISTERED with the copyright office. Go to <copyright.gov> and the necessary forms are available there. You want the one for a text document. Note, also, that crediting authorship is a plagiarism issue, not a copyright issue. Plagiarism is an ethical dilemma, while copyright infringement is a legal one.

Protected or Not? | Document Protection

? *We have created a document and want to keep ownership of it and not allow every district to copy the materials. What can we do to protect this document? Is there a statement that will assure us that it cannot be copied, reproduced, or distributed?*

© You don't need to do a thing. This document is automatically protected by copyright with all the rights thereto pertaining. If you would like to be able to provide some punch, register this document with the copyright office in Washington <www.loc.gov/copyright/>. It costs $30, but if the copyright is infringed, you can then sue for damages. Of course, if you just want to alert folks to the fact that you do not wish to allow unlimited reproduction of the document, add a statement like: "This document is protected by copyright. No reproduction, distribution, or adaptation is permitted without prior permission from the copyright holder." (Then add your address, e-mail, or phone number.)

Student Work | Displaying Student Work

? *Can a teacher display student work in the classroom or hallways?*

© Displaying student work in the classroom is no problem because it is part of the educational experience directly related to classroom work. It is also only displayed to students and teachers in the class. The further you get from the classroom the more public the display. Remember that the student owns the copyright in his own work. If the student did all the work, and you get permission from the parents (for minor students), you should be okay on any public display. If the student used portions of copyrighted works in his work, the student cannot give permission for that which he doesn't own.

? *Is it okay for a teacher to ask for permission to display student work and the parents agree? Or, can a teacher send a letter home at the beginning of a school year, which covers them for a whole year, and ask permission of them to display student work in the classroom and hallway? Must a teacher ask for permission each time he/she wishes to display any student work?*

© For work that the student did entirely, a yearlong permission should work for in-school display. Display in the classroom should not be a copyright issue (other parental preferences, notwithstanding) because of the educational exemptions given for students. For broader display (like a literary magazine, Web page, etc.), you want a signed permission form listing each work. Remember, student work that uses significant copyrighted materials requires a fair use assessment. In the case of multimedia work, for example, the multimedia fair use guidelines would apply. For something like a literary work, you should assess using the four tests of fair use. If the work will become property of the school (as in a published literary magazine, newspaper, or mural) transfer of the student's copyright must be in writing. Consult an intellectual property attorney for appropriate contractual language.

Student Work | Online Worksheets

? *Can a teacher put workbook sheets online for students who are absent? We have paid for the right to copy them. The Web site would be password protected. Would it be okay if they were online for a limited time?*

© This is a TEACH Act (Technology, Education, and Copyright Harmonization Act) question. Under certain restrictions, materials can be put online, behind a password. The key thing here though is that these are "consumables." The TEACH Act prohibits digitizing materials that are consumable. The other key factor is that you have a license to reproduce. You need to examine that license VERY carefully looking for conditions that restrict digital reproduction and/or transmission. If the contract is silent on those issues, you should contact the producer from whom you got the license. Be explicit about what rights you wish to license. In the absence of language stating you have permission to digitize and distribute, a court would look to the intention of the parties involved to interpret the contract. Without explicit discussions on digital distribution rights, a court would likely find it difficult to side with the school in such a case.

Work for Hire | Copyright of Q and A

? *A teacher friend and I have begun writing units of study based on a set of books about the world's greatest artists. We started by writing questions with answers based on information from these books. For example, the students read the book about Claude Monet, and answer five or six questions that we have written in the state academic assessment format. Then we do an art project, and ultimately have a big art show at the end of the year. Our principal has suggested we conduct some workshops for teachers in our school district. If this situation expands into other districts, which we think it may, we feel that it is in our best interest to start charging for the units of study that we have developed. What are the copyright regulations concerning a situation like this?*

© The problem that I see with this scenario is that you two teachers don't own what you have created. They were created for your classes, within the scope of your employment. So the units belong to the SCHOOL DISTRICT, not to you. This is a classic work-for-hire situation. You first want to get IN WRITING acknowledgment from the District that they make no claim on your creations.

That being cleared up, simply asking state assessment-type questions that can be answered from this book series or other sources does not infringe the copyright of the book when you just mention that the book can be used to find the answer to the question, as long as other similar sources have comparable information. Remember that facts are not protected by copyright: only the expression of those facts is protected.

Work for Hire | Copyright of Teacher Made Materials

? *Does "work made for hire" mean an employee may not own his own work if he was doing work he was employed to do? A teacher should be able to put together lesson plans, work sheets, etc. that are totally original work, without the school having any part in the copyright. Does the teacher need to have some type of clearance from her employer/school before publishing such work?*

© Barring some agreement that a teacher owns the rights to everything created, the school could make a case that materials created for the teacher's class would be considered "work for hire." However, if the teacher is teaching fifth grade, but writes a symphony that is ultimately performed by the high school orchestra, that would likely NOT be considered work for hire because the work was not created "within the scope of employment." Many schools don't care to claim copyright on works created by teachers, but it is always safe (and many publishers, including Linworth Publishing) will demand verification that the work is free to publish.

Work for Hire | School Organization Logo

? *A school organization designed a logo for use on sweatshirts, etc., with an organization officer doing all of the work. After a falling out between the officer and the rest of the school community, the officer quit. She now claims she owns the copyright of the logo and will not allow them to order sweatshirts with the logo. Since the logo was created for the organization, does the organization own the copyright or does the ex-officer who did the work?*

© Unless the president was PAID by the organization (and therefore the work would likely be work for hire) or she had some contract, express or implied, that the organization owned the work, the former officer does own the copyright in the work. Of course, the organization could hire a lawyer and fight this, but that would make it a VERY expensive logo. I'd suggest coming up with a new design.

Work for Hire | Web Page Ownership

? *I designed our library's Web page, which is linked from the school's home page. The library page is hosted on a server independent of the school's service. The artwork is original and I work on the page daily on my own time (not school time) in the evenings and on weekends. Who owns the page?*

© This is a good question—and one that has yet to be settled by the courts. There's a good case to be made for the idea that your Web page is "within the scope of your employment," hence could be considered a work for hire with the district that owns the copyright. Work that you do for your classes (even if done at home) can be claimed by your district as their intellectual property, although many districts choose not to. In addition, if you've put the school's name on the page, thus implying that this is an official school page, school officials could make a good case that they own the entity so represented, and you're misrepresenting this page as belonging to the school if you claim personal ownership. Unfortunately, the only point in your favor is that your site is hosted independently. For specific legal advice, you need to consult with an attorney who specializes in intellectual property matters.

Work for Hire | Work Hired by School

? *While on a year's leave of absence, my principal called to ask if I would work with at-risk kids in 3rd grade on a part-time basis. She also asked me if I would write some tests for 3rd and 4th grade using the new state standardized test format. I wrote approximately 12 tests and am interested in knowing how I could copyright them.*

© Since you were hired by the school to write these materials, you cannot copyright them. The school owns the copyright under the work for hire rules. Since you were paid to create these materials, the person who paid you owns the copyright unless you have a contract that assigns the copyright to you.

Chapter Two

Print Materials

P rint materials are the foundation of schoolwork and the impetus for the first educational explanations of fair use after the last significant revision of U.S. copyright law. The report of the Kastenmeier Committee after the 1976 copyright law revision gave concrete interpretation to the intent of Congress about what they meant—in school terms—by the very obtuse fair use section of the new law. Fortunately for educators, the Report gives specific guidance in quantitative terms about how many pages, articles, chapters, and images that a teacher may use in class during a year or term.

Unfortunately, the educational guidelines don't address many NON-instructional school uses. A significant number of activities occur in a typical K-12 building that are part of the school experience but don't meet the "direct teach" requirement that is needed for the print guidelines to apply. In such cases, the statutory four tests of fair use are the ones to apply. Since this book only deals with questions and answers please refer to the companion *Copyright for Schools, 4th Edition* (Linworth Publishing, Inc., 2005) or any comprehensive copyright manual for specifics on the two methods of assessing fair use of print materials.

Fair Use | Audio Copies of Books

? *We need to make an audio copy of a summer-reading book for a group of special needs students. Can anyone make audiotapes for use with special needs people and, if so, what qualifies as "special needs"? We have many "classified" students that could benefit from reading along with a text, but not all are specifically dyslexic.*

© It is still not legal to make your own audiobooks under most circumstances. However, the organizations that record books for blind and dyslexic people are able to make these tapes under a special exception to copyright for these groups. The patrons must be diagnosed as unable to use standard print works. Anyone who qualifies under these conditions can get the special tape players free from their state library or the Library of Congress. The recordings must be made on special, slow-speed recorders so that the tapes cannot be played in standard tape players. Get the forms to be certified for this use from LOC or your state library; these organizations also may be able to provide the tapes at no cost.

Fair Use | Audio Recording of Book Chapters

? *A teacher in our district has suggested that we have volunteers read and record (on audiotape) books from our elementary library for use by ESL students. Is this a violation of copyright law? If no audiobook is published for the title, is this permissible? Are there any conditions under which this type of recording would be permitted?*

© Such copying is permitted in only one instance; the end user (student) must be identified as handicapped (unable to use traditional print because of some handicap) and the handicap status verified by a medical professional. The student must be able to qualify for the services of the Library of Congress National Library Service for the Blind and Physically Handicapped (see <http://www.loc.gov/nls/eligible.html> for eligibility criteria). The recording may then be made, but only on equipment supplied for recording for the blind: a 4-track recorder using a 15/16 ips speed (NOT commercial cassette recorders). The fact that a book may not be available on tape is not a consideration in the legal specifications. Since the Recording for the Blind services are done on a request basis, be sure to make your arrangements early to be certain to have the materials in time for your expected use.

Fair Use | Audio Recording of Books

? *One of our world history teachers and an assistant principal want to start a service project whereby honors students will record the chapters of a textbook on to audiotapes. Students who are "challenged" readers could then play the tapes as they read along in the textbook, thus improving reading skills and comprehension of text materials. Each student has his own copy of the textbook.*

Here's where the copyright question comes in: the publisher of the textbook offers audiotapes that summarize the chapters, but not tapes that read the chapters word for word. Also, we cannot afford to purchase these tapes. Would this be a copyright violation? If not, could the tapes be checked out to students to take home?

 Under current copyright law, the only way you can make the tapes is if you meet these conditions:

- A physician must verify that the students are unable to use standard print. This verification must be made to the Library of Congress Division of Blind and Physically Handicapped or to your State Library's similar division.

- The recordings must be made on special recorders provided by these two sources and must NOT be playable on regular consumer-type recorders.

You have an alternative. Your local Recording for the Blind and Dyslexic may be able to provide the recordings you want. They make special licensing agreements for these types of uses. That will get you the tapes, but it won't involve your honors students.

That's about it for your options, unless you write to the publishing company and get WRITTEN permission to make your own tapes. A bit of good news is that most publishing companies will provide audio copies of their textbooks for use with special needs students, or your state Department of Education has audio copies available of adopted textbooks. Contact them first.

Fair Use | Comic Superheroes

? *Our student council plans to use famous comic book characters in this year's "Teachers are Superheroes" theme. They will create posters with these characters and display them around the building. Is this use "fair use"?*

© Students using (copying) works of art (including cartoons) for their personal use to become better artists is fair as long as the copies remain with the student and the work is kept private. Your situation does not involve direct teaching, so you have lost the educational exemption there. However, as with all uses of copyrighted materials, you can do a standard fair use assessment on the situation:

- Nonprofit is good, but this isn't criticism, commentary, or news reporting. It isn't educational either. ("Educational" is best explained by substituting the idea of direct teaching.)

- The work is creative, but it is published, so that is a split. (Creative works are controlled more strictly; published works are more freely usable than unpublished ones.) I don't know how much of the work you are using, so I can't guess on this one. You may be doing an adaptation, which could be even more "if-y."

- You are making the copy to avoid paying for clip art, or other licensed art, which is not good. (Such use impacts the market for the work or licensing of the work. Any time you take money out of someone's pocket, the fair use assessment does not generally fall in your favor.)

In addition, the characters are trademarked and trademarks are highly protected. I would recommend the students contact the comic syndicate or the publisher—whoever owns the copyright. I know that many of the comic book publishers are almost as litigious as Disney is, so contacting them is a good plan. In the alternative, you can have an artistic student draw some type of superhero, and use that with just a slight adjustment in the campaign.

Chapter Two: Print Materials

Fair Use | Copies of Song Lyrics

? *May teachers make copies for each student of just the lyrics from a song for a specific activity if the activity involves face-to-face teaching?*

© Consider song lyrics to be a poem, and apply the print guidelines for poetry. Remember that such duplication can occur only once. Repeated use of these lyrics in subsequent years or terms will always require permission. Also, if one knows far enough in advance (approximately four to six weeks) that the lyrics will be used, there is sufficient time to receive permission, so a request for permission is in order. If one would have time to get permission, permission is always required. If the permission doesn't arrive by the date of the first expected use, use the lyrics ONCE under the fair use exemption. Any use in subsequent semesters or terms will require permission.

Fair Use | *Copying Educational Periodicals*

? *Our district office subscribes to many educational periodicals. The title pages are copied and circulated to all district school libraries. Teachers circle the titles they want, and the articles are copied at the district office and sent to them. The district office could be copying the same article for all schools each month. Since this periodical is bought for the district, is this against copyright law? Is the district office limited to the five-copy rule for issues less than five years old?*

© This practice is suspect. In fact, even copying the table of contents is protected. You could retype it or otherwise extract the information, but you can't make photocopies of it and distribute it without permission or payment of royalties. Call Copyright Clearance Center and ask what they will charge for each table of contents. The cost may surprise you. Each of your libraries is bound by the Rule of Five. Each should subscribe if it requests more than five reprints per periodical title per year.

Fair Use | Copying to Substitute for Textbooks

? *A teacher has 20 students in one class, and another teacher has about that many students in a different class. Both teach the same course. They have 22 books total for this many students. They want the students to get information from the texts, but will not send the texts home. The teachers asked if they could copy certain pages (many pages throughout the book) so the students can use them at home. Today one of the teachers asked if it's permissible to allow the students to scan in the pages they need, and then take the copies home to study. If there was one book available in the library, and the students came in and asked for copies from that book, would it then be all right? The teachers are trying to avoid buying extra texts.*

© You are correct in your assessment. This is to avoid purchasing legitimate copies of the book (a black mark on factor four of the fair use guidelines). Take a look at the print guidelines. They say the teacher can make multiple copies of a single chapter of a book. This sounds like much more than a chapter. I can't see any way this proposal would be legitimate. Even putting the book in the library and telling the students to make copies would be "top down" copying, which is prohibited. There is nothing on your side here in the four-test fair use analysis, other than you are an educational institution. That alone is not enough to make the use fair.

Fair Use | Copying Workbooks

? *If a student loses his workbook, can the teacher make a copy for him, or can she copy some pages for him? The teacher pointed out that the original workbook had been purchased but lost.*

© The only time you can make copies of consumables is if an unused replacement copy is no longer available at a "reasonable cost." So, if the student loses the workbook, he needs to buy a replacement. However, once the order is sent off for the replacement, the teacher can make page-by-page copies until the replacement arrives. Remember, nothing in copyright law says that books (or workbooks) will last forever. If they are lost or damaged and replacements are available, there is nothing in the law to protect you from having to purchase a replacement.

Fair Use | Copyright Clearance Center Charges

? *I recently e-mailed a publisher for permission to reprint multiple copies of a 38-page article and then found the Copyright Clearance Center Web site. I entered the needed information into the CCC's online form. I received the messages "title permission granted" and "base fee: 0.00, per page fee: .200." Am I supposed to pay a fee to reproduce?*

© Yes. CCC will always charge you money for permissions. In this case, they want 20 cents per page for each page of each copy, or $7.60 for each article. You can recover that cost from the students, but you may not charge beyond the actual cost of the copies (the copyright fee plus actual photocopy charges). The clearance center thinks they are being nice by not charging you any "base fee." A base fee would be something like $20 plus 20 cents per page.

Now that you have registered that copy request with CCC, they will be expecting money from you. If you decide not to make the copies under this license, you need to let them know. According to their file of Frequently Asked Questions, you can cancel a permission request any time during the permission process. For a canceled request, you pay only the minimum processing charge of $1 per item. However, you may not cancel any request that has already been invoiced.

Fair Use | Copyright of Famous Speeches

? *Every year our school hosts a school-wide patriotic speech festival. The participants choose and memorize a speech from a list of competition selections. The choices include Patrick Henry's "Give me liberty or give me death" speech, Franklin Roosevelt's "War Address to Congress," and many more speeches from all periods of American history. Rather than print thick packets of 40 famous speeches for each student, we would like to make them available online. In that way students could simply print their chosen speech, and we will save reams of paper. Does copyright law allow the posting of speeches on our external school Web site? I realize that many of the speeches are in the public domain, but how about the late 20th century speeches? What is the cut-off date for public domain entry, or is that even a relevant question? Would it be advisable to post links to speeches rather than post the speeches themselves?*

© Patrick Henry's speech is now in the public domain (if it were ever protected). Official speeches and writings of U.S. presidents and officials are also public domain by law, because they are employees of the U.S. government. Speeches of private individuals are protected by copyright if they are published after 1923. Some works before 1978 may have fallen into the public domain due to lack of registration or other flukes of pre-1978 copyright, so you will need to do an assessment of each speech to determine copyright status before posting. A link to those copyright-protected speeches would be more appropriate than re-posting the work, assuming the site where the work is posted has permission to post it.

Fair Use | *Fair Use vs. License*

? *The Speech and Debate team would like to make several copies of numerous pages from books that state, "No portion of this book may be reproduced or copied without written permission of …." Is this "fair use"?*

© A notice in a book cannot override federal law regarding fair use. However, a signed contract or license can. It is impossible to answer the question without knowing the book, where it came from, how it was acquired, etc. etc. Here are some things to consider. Copying for classroom use, in limited amounts as suggested in the print guidelines, is permissible. Going far beyond that limit is probably NOT fair use. This appears to be, from the description in your question, an extracurricular use. In that case, all of the classroom guidelines go out the window and you fall back on standard fair use—the four tests. You have to consider if this work is creative, if it is published, if the use is nonprofit, how much of the work you are using, and what effect the use will have on the market for or value of the work. HOWEVER, if you have licensed these materials, and the license says they can't be copied, all bets are off. The license controls.

Fair Use | *Fill-in-the-Blank Textbooks*

? *A teacher wants to type a couple of pages out of a textbook and leave important words out putting blanks instead. She wants the students to read the textbook and fill in the blanks on the page she's typed up. (I think this is mainly so she'll know they read the pages.) It would be less than 10% of the work, but she's changing the format.*

© This use is easily fair, but it can't be repeated from term to term with the same work without permission, just as with any copying situation. One time only under fair use. My question would be if she plans to do that repeatedly from the text throughout the year, or is this a one-time thing? If this is a teaching technique she plans to employ, she might want to discuss it with the textbook publisher. They may have some arrangement with your state or district for adopted texts that will allow such uses.

Fair Use | *Folktales*

? *Is there a problem with using a story someone has copyrighted (mostly versions of folktales) to create a script for a play? When I find a really good version of a tale, I like to use a lot of the text, the character names, etc., but I fear this may be a copyright no-no.*

© Although the original fairy tales (Grimm) are public domain, they are public domain only in the original form. Anyone's retelling or translation of the tale is protected under the copyright laws in force at the time of publication. Their expression of the tale is protected by copyright. You state that you like to use a "lot of the text" and you are creating an adaptation for public performance. You are correct to be concerned.

Fair Use | ILL Copying

? *How many articles from each issue of a periodical is a library allowed to copy for interlibrary loan?*

© The providing library may make any copies requested by other organizations since it is the *requesting* library's responsibility to maintain copyright compliance according to the CONTU guidelines.

Fair Use | Is the Bible Public Domain?

? *Is the Bible considered public domain? Is it protected under copyright law? If it is protected by copyright, who would own the copyright?*

© The answer depends on the version. The King James Version is in the public domain. New translations may still be protected. Check the copyright date of the version you are using. Anything copyrighted before 1923 is public domain. Watch out for "enhanced" versions though. The Bible text itself may be public domain, but the notes, among other things, may still be protected.

Fair Use | Kurzweil Scanners

? *We purchased a license for Kurzweil 300 scan/read CD-ROMs to be used in 12 of our special education classrooms. The teachers are taking books and scanning them using this program. The students, using a computer, listen to what has been scanned. Is this a copyright infringement?*

© As long as the students using these copies are blind or physically handicapped (unable to use standard books because of physical disability) this is permitted in the new exemption for the handicapped (HR 3754, Public Law 104-197).

Fair Use | Legal Sources of Reading Passages

? *Our special education campus coordinator must gather reading at a specific grade level to use as practice for our state academic assessment. She knows that we have rights to materials from past administrations of the assessment, but she would like to know if there are any other legal sources of reading passages we can use to compile into a practice workbook for the upcoming test.*

© You can always use passages for your own classroom under fair use. You can use the print guidelines with their limits (which only allow a one-time use) or you can fall back on the four tests of fair use. If you plan to use these documents repeatedly, you probably would rather use the fair use analysis than the print guidelines.

For the four-test analysis, you know you are okay as a nonprofit educational institution, but that won't work for those of you in for-profit situations like Edison schools, some private schools and tutoring services like Sylvan, and day-care centers.

The works you will be copying may be factual, in which case you are fine on that assessment too. If the work is a literary passage, that is creative, so that part of this factor would count against you. However, this second factor is a two-parter: is the work published? If it is published, that mitigates the first half somewhat. So for a typical literary passage, this factor would be a wash.

The third factor is how much you are going to use. That is an important consideration. A paragraph out of a book like *Holes* is insignificant. A similar amount from a picture book might be half the book! The less you are going to use the better in most cases.

The final factor is what effect your use will have on the market for the work or the value of the work you are using. Taking a paragraph or two out of a novel isn't likely to impact sales of the book or the reputation of the book. It isn't likely to prevent sales of reprints like copying a complete article would. This factor is weighed very heavily if you plan to make broad distribution of your practice tests, say district-wide, or if you put the questions into district curriculum that your district distributes to other districts or sells to other districts (a growing phenomenon). So consider that angle here.

Once you have done the four assessments, you can figure your risk for each individual question.

Fair Use | Lending a Bound Periodical

? *Are there any copyright restrictions on lending an entire bound periodical volume to another school?*

© If you are talking about *physically* sending the magazine to another school, there are no restrictions on that form of interlibrary loan (ILL). The ILL guidelines are for ILL *copying*.

Fair Use | Movie Scripts Online

? *Our drama teacher wants to use a script from an online site for her classes. The production will later become a public performance at the school. This site has scripts that are rewrites of popular movies, but the site does not indicate that any permission has been granted from the producers. The school principal is questioning the teacher's use of these scripts for her classroom and/or performance.*

© Using things such as this for public performance are just disasters looking for a place to happen, especially if you advertise it. Using a movie script in class would probably be fair use EXCEPT that you have reason to believe that this copy could be illegal. Fair use is always predicated on a legal copy. And the reason the teacher is using these scripts rather than purchasing commercial copies is to deprive the producer of a sale, right? If you have a board policy requiring copyright compliance, that is probably the basis for your principal's (commendable) concern.

Fair Use | *Nine Instances of Multiple Copying*

? *I don't understand the "Nine Instances of Multiple Copying." Where are the rules listed for this? Can we only make multiple copies for students up to nine times during a semester/year if we're copying a chapter of a book, essay, article, or short poem? What about using any of the copies again (recycling so we don't waste paper) without seeking publisher's rights?*

© It is part of the Kastenmeier report returned in 1976. We refer to those as the print guidelines. It is the same report where they discuss multiple copying for classroom use and single copies for teachers. In that report (this is a Congressional committee) they put the two-page limit on copying picture books and prohibit copying consumable materials. Look on page eight of Circular 21 from the copyright office at <www.copyright.gov/circs/circ21.pdf>. When you make multiple copies for students, the guidelines tell you that the copies must go to the students because they specifically say you can't "accumulate" the copies, and you can't copy the same item again in a subsequent term. So yes, if you need the same material copied semester after semester (for one-semester classes) or year after year (for full-year classes) you need to purchase the rights or get permission.

Fair Use | *Out-of-Print Book Copies*

? *Our music teacher wants to make a classroom set of copies from out-of-print books. The author is deceased, and the publishing company has gone out of business. However, every page carries a copyright notice. The teacher really wants to use the material and would buy a classroom set if he could. Under the circumstances, can he copy the material?*

© The teacher is out of luck unless he can find the successors to the publishing company. Out-of-print does not equal out-of-copyright. The Library of Congress can help you trace the copyright holder, as can the Copyright Clearance Center <http://www.copyright.com/>. Remember to look to see if the book was published when copyright renewal was still required. You may be lucky and find that the copyright was not renewed and this material has fallen into the public domain for non-renewal.

Fair Use | Photocopies of Internet Pages

? *I print out pages from the Internet, photocopy them, and pass them along to my department heads. I usually include a note for them to share this with members of their department. Can I legally print out pages from the Internet by invoking the Netscape or Explorer print function? Under the fair use you can make a SINGLE copy of up to a chapter of a book or an article of a magazine (not the entire work) for your own PERSONAL use and education, including use in teaching. Can I legally photocopy these pages that I printed?*

© Not without permission if the copies are not for your personal use or you have not been requested to make the copies. These teachers aren't your students so you don't qualify for the educational fair use exemption. (If they were your students you would have some limited ability to make multiple copies.) You will need permission to make the copies you describe.

? *Can other teachers make copies of what I send out?*

© No. They are going to have to make their own copy, and then evaluate the fair use exemption regarding the uses they plan.

Fair Use | Poster Making

? *We have a poster-making machine. It will take an 8½" X 11" copy or printout and make it into a 23" x 31" poster. If a teacher makes a copy of a page out of a textbook and uses the copy to make a poster with this machine for display in the classroom during the unit being taught, is he violating any copyright laws?*

© Well, a single copy of something for personal research or for use in teaching is okay, so if the teacher discards the original photocopy and just keeps the poster, I think he would have a reasonable claim of fair use.

Fair Use | Presenting Student Work at a Conference

? *Can I present student work at a conference (I am not making a profit? I demonstrate how our students are using multimedia integrated into the curriculum.*

© Absolutely not. Students may demonstrate material under fair use, but only to show it to other students and teachers in the class. The students then own the copyright on the portion of the material they created, but not on the parts demonstrated under fair use. You cannot present that work without permission from the student. You also cannot retain copies of student work that contains copies made under fair use. These copies must revert to the student. Note that "student" is defined as someone in a degree-granting institution, i.e., enrolled for credit in a public or private nonprofit elementary or secondary school or college. Workshop presenters have no fair use exemption—even if the participants are teachers in nonprofit schools.

Fair Use | Proof of Sources

? A teacher is concerned about cheating/plagiarism in class. Therefore, students are required to turn in copies of all sources cited in a paper due at the end of the semester. Is this REQUIREMENT a violation of fair use of copied (printed) materials?

© The fact that the teacher is directing the copying is the tripping issue here. Under the print guidelines this would probably not fly. However, if they are just making copies of a bit of a work (the part they used, plus the title page, perhaps) that would likely qualify under a normal fair use analysis. The key issue here is that the copies must vest with the student. The teacher can request to see them, but can't keep the copies. To be even more scrupulous, the teacher could demand to see the original sources. The student has the option to make photocopies or drag the books/magazines in to class. Which one do you think the student would choose? The key is that it is the student's choice and isn't directed from above.

Fair Use | *Publishing Student Work*

? *A fifth grade teacher had her students write a story using their favorite characters from their favorite books as the main character. She wanted to use this technique so students would analyze the characterization and maintain the personality, motives, and physical traits of the character to learn about the reciprocal nature of reading and writing. Now she would like to use one of the papers as part of her National Board portfolio. Would this be fair use? Should she explain in her narrative that this work was done under fair use?*

© Teachers can certainly do this type of derivative work as a classroom activity, but I don't recommend publishing the results or you might be sued. Someone who used the *Gone with the Wind* characters and retold the tale from the point of view of the slaves was recently sued. However, the STUDENTS own the copyright in their own work, and the teacher may not appropriate that work without permission of the student or his parents (if the student is a minor). If the Board portfolio is not published on the Web, and the teacher has permission to use the student work, the limited use described here would likely be reasonable.

Fair Use | Recording Books on Audiotape

? *A teacher plans to have students make audiotapes of published children's books and then loan the tapes to teachers at our school through the library. Is this permissible?*

© Only under the following circumstances may you make the types of records you describe: The recordings must be for *identified handicapped individuals*. Basically, a medical professional must certify that the student is unable to use traditional print materials.

The recording must be made on a machine specified for recording for the blind. Commercial or consumer recording equipment *must not be able to play* these recordings.

Understand that making an audio copy of a book (also called a "phonorecord") is exactly the same, as far as the law goes, as making a photocopy of a book. There is no fair use to make complete photocopies of books, so why would there be a free use to make audio copies? Duplication of the recordings compounds the infringement, as does distribution of the copies. There are many factors weighing in against you.

Fair Use | Recording Books on Tape

? *A teacher, unbeknownst to the librarian, had her daughters read books on tape and place them in the literacy room for teachers' use with classes. The teachers check the tapes out with the books, but it is not from the library. The newspaper printed this practice in a positive article about volunteerism. Am I correct that this is a violation of copyright? If it is a violation, how do we correct it besides removing the tapes?*

© Yes, it is a violation. Making audio copies is okay if there is a documented disability (including dyslexia) and you have a physician statement to that effect, but the law (Title 17, Chapter 1, Section 121) limits the type of recording to those players that are suitable for the blind—those that you get from the Library of Congress or the state library. Basically it was enacted to protect Recording for the Blind and Dyslexic, etc., from copyright suits. You have to have the special players (15/16 ips, much slower than standard players). I'd recommend you remove and destroy all the tapes, and provide remedial training to the staff. Make it sign-off training so you can document.

Fair Use | Recording Picture Books

? *Is it okay for a teacher to record a picture book and let kindergarten students listen to the story on the tape while looking at the book?*

© There is a special exception to copyright law for handicapped users that allows this practice, but the person for whom you are recording the book must be blind or otherwise physically unable to use a book. Making a copy of a book by recording it is the same (according to the law) as making a copy by photocopying it. Remember that for a picture book there is a copy limitation (under fair use) of two pages or 10% of the text, whichever is less.

Fair Use | Reproducible Magazines

? *Some librarians have been told they should no longer subscribe to reproducible magazines for teachers in their schools because of the caveats contained in such publications. One caveat says, "Permission is granted to the original subscriber to reproduce pages for individual classroom use only and not for resale or distribution. Reproductions for an entire school or school system are prohibited." Another's wording is even worse: "All material in this journal . . . may be photocopied for instructional use by the original subscriber and for the non-commercial purpose of educational or scientific advancement. It may not be photocopied for instructional use by second parties other than the original subscriber without prior permission." This sounds like the publications don't want libraries to make the issues available to teachers and others for legitimate educational purposes. Does this fall under the right-of-first-sale rule?*

© No, the right of first sale doesn't apply in this instance, because you aren't disposing of the original, you're just proposing to copy it. I have a letter from one of those magazines clarifying its position, however. They state that it's perfectly okay for libraries to subscribe, and for *individual* teachers to make class copies of activities. What they object to is copies being made for an entire grade-level or school. They say that as long as an individual teacher is making the decision and making the copies (or requesting that copies be made on her behalf), the use is fair. I would interpret the second statement in that vein, as well.

Chapter Two: Print Materials **49**

Fair Use | *Rule of Five*

? *For interlibrary loan (ILL), can a library request five articles from each issue of a given periodical?*

© The Rule of Five states that during the current calendar year you may request up to five copies of articles from the last four calendar years of a periodical title. It makes no difference from whom you request the articles or from which issues within that four-year window the articles come. The five articles can all be from the same issue, or all from different issues. As long as the requested articles are within the four-year window, they will count against your allotment of five.

Fair Use | Student Cookbook

? *My PTO wants to put together a student cookbook to sell for a fundraiser. Students didn't give the source of the recipes so the PTO doesn't know, and doubts, if the recipes are original. How can we best handle the copyright of those recipes that probably came from Betty Crocker or some other cookbook?*

© The good news is that simple lists of ingredients and minimal directions are not protected by copyright. Only some unique wording or narrative that is part of the recipe is minimally protected by copyright. Because your students have likely been creative with their recipe directions (as only kids can be), there is probably little problem with your recipe book.

Fair Use | *Student-Made Anthologies*

? *Our tenth grade English teachers require their students to create an anthology of poetry, essays, short stories, and articles on one thematic aspect of the Holocaust. Since the law states that copying should not be used to create or be a substitute for anthologies, compilations, or collective works, is this a violation of copyright law?*

© The print anthologies restriction is addressed more to teachers who simply photocopy the world rather than purchase textbooks. If the students make only a single copy of the materials for their own projects, make the choice of what to copy, and the projects revert to the students at the end of the assignment, there should be no problem.

Fair Use | Taping Books for Special Education

? *A special education teacher tapes popular books for her high school students. It is a technique encouraged by a particular reading program. I told her it was a copyright violation, because it denied the copyright holders the rights to any derivative creations of their original works. Both she and I called the reading program headquarters and were told that it was not a copyright infringement. I called the Association of American Publishers and a publisher of one of the books the teacher wanted to tape. They both said it was a copyright infringement.*

© If the students are unable to use standard print because of a handicap (including dyslexia), a teacher can tape the books as an assist for students who are having trouble reading. The tapes must conform to the specifications set forth in Section 121 of U.S. copyright law.

Fair Use | Vertical Files

? *I am an elementary librarian at three schools and have a vertical file in each library. Is it legal for students and teachers to make a copy or copies of vertical file materials on the library copier?*

© Yes, a student or teacher can make a single copy of an article for personal or educational use. The problem is making copies to PUT IN the vertical file, such as your making a copy of an article at School A to put in the vertical file at Schools B & C.

Fair Use | Worksheets on the Web

? *A teacher asked if she could put the worksheet that goes with her Spanish textbook on her Web site when she puts lessons on the Web site. I told her that the company would probably give permission if she asked. Was I right?*

© I seriously doubt they would give permission. Remember, not only are you copying a consumable (something that is barred by the print guidelines), but you are also digitizing it and distributing (and displaying) it to the world! Not bad: violating four of the six reserved rights in one fell swoop! Now, if that Web site is password protected, you MIGHT get a different result under the TEACH Act, but even TEACH is touchy about consumables. After all, selling copies to students year after year is how consumables publishers make their money. When you digitize the pages, and share them with the world, you are taking money right out of the pocket of the publishers. They tend to get understandably upset when they find out.

Public Display | Puppet Show Adaptations

Note: "Public display" in this context means allowing people who are not members of a family and its immediate circle of friends to view a print work. Virtually any activity that occurs in a public school that involves print materials would be a public display.

? *We have some teachers who often use a book as the basis for a puppet show or student "play." Is it permissible to do this, assuming we meet the other criteria for fair use in an educational setting? What about a class performing their play for another group of students in the school? Should we contact the publisher and get permission?*

© The only permitted fair use performance of a book is in a non-dramatic performance. By making a puppet play out of it, you have adapted the work dramatically and performed it publicly. Adaptation and/or dramatization are not included in the fair use allowances. You would need permission.

Chapter Three

Graphic Materials

If a picture is worth a thousand words, to a graphic artist or photographer it is worth a thousand dollars. Well, maybe more. It is how the graphic artist pays the rent. Artists, illustrators, and photographers have the same rights, under copyright law, to profit from their creative expression, however the average person never considers the artist whose work enhances, illuminates, or decorates the works they read. Graphics abound within print works, as well as having a life of their own in art galleries and photo studios. Images are the whole reason for the graphical Web, yet when most people consider asking permission to use materials or doing a fair use analysis of materials, graphics are largely ignored.

When doing an analysis of graphic materials, one of the sticking points is generally how much of the item you plan to use. It is uncommon for someone to use only a portion of a graphical work. Ten percent of a picture is usually of interest only to other artists examining details of technique. Those who want to use a photo or image on a Web page, for instance, usually want the whole image. Adding insult to injury is the fact that almost all graphic materials are creative by definition. From the beginning the person doing a fair use analysis is down for half of the fair use questions. The answers to the remaining two factors had best be very strong to achieve a favorable outcome.

Fortunately, there are a few school-specific exemptions for use of graphic materials in direct teaching situations. The multimedia guidelines, the TEACH Act (for Web use), and the print guidelines offer limited use of graphic materials. See *Copyright for Schools: A Practical Guide, 4th Edition* (Linworth Publishing, Inc., 2005), or any other general copyright reference work for details.

Fair Use | Art Masterpiece Museum Brochure

? *Our library buys airbrushed reproductions of great art masterpieces from a company. We display them in the library and circulate them to the schools. The art teacher asked a student to create a brochure that has a photograph of the painting and gives a brief summary of each artist exhibited in the display. The information was obtained from various Internet sites. The art teacher claims this information is "common knowledge" and there is no need to cite our sources. She says she has been to museums all over the world and there is never a "works cited" included on the brochure.*

© The item copyrighted in the museum brochure is the PHOTOGRAPH of the painting, probably not the painting itself since likely it was painted before 1923. If the museum takes the photos, it owns the images and can use them without citing them (that's why the art teacher hasn't seen citations in art museum brochures and why museums won't let you take photos). The person writing the text in the museum brochure is likely an expert on that artist who would not need to refer to other sources to produce the text. Your student, however, is not such an expert.

There has been a court ruling that thumbnails (tiny images that refer to sites that carry real images) are fair use. Of course, your images in your brochure aren't thumbnails technically, since they don't link to a legal copy of the image. So, you might need permission for the images in the brochure if the paintings were done after 1923 because you are using the whole image, it is creative, and you are not able to claim classroom use, as this isn't for a specific class. Works painted before 1923 would be in the public domain.

The written matter in the brochure may be the copyright of the student who wrote it (in which case he should be acknowledged) or it may be lifted from the Web pages referenced, in which case it must be acknowledged both as a copyright and a plagiarism defense. Citing sources is good scholarship as well as appropriate copyright practice.

Fair Use | Citing Book Covers

? *In discussing with middle school students the copyright issues in copying and pasting book cover art from the likes of BWI or Amazon, or even scanning it from their own book, how should they cite things like this? Do they cite the Web site from which the image was pulled, or cite the author of the book or even the illustrator? How about if the image was photographed directly? What issues are involved if one archives these papers on a Web site?*

© Just as with all materials, you cite the creator of what you are using, then where you found it. So the cover art would be by the artist (note that the book illustrator does not always create the cover art), then the title and publisher, then "available online at: http://...." (Or whatever is the appropriate indication of online location for the style sheet you are using). If you scan the book cover yourself from the source, you just cite the source you scanned from, though with the artist as the creator.

The issue with archiving these sorts of things on a Web site is that while students do have a fair use right to use limited amounts of materials for their own research and education, they do not have the right to redistribute those materials to the world. Putting something on the Web is the equivalent to worldwide redistribution. There have been several recent cases where student fans of authors have created fan Web sites with scanned images and excerpts, and the authors and their publishers have taken high offense and demanded the sites be taken down. While a good attorney might be able to make a viable case for fair use, citing criticism and commentary for the use, the cost of fighting the potential lawsuit would fall on the student (or in this case the school). Depending on how risk-averse you are you might not want to take that chance.

Fair Use | *Clip Art*

? *We are designing Web pages for our middle school and want to spice them up with some clip art. If I purchase a CD-ROM of clip art, can we legally use it on our Web site, or must we use only public domain clip art? Can other teachers on my campus use my clip-art* CD *for their own products such as newsletters and worksheets?*

© You will need to check the license that came with your clip art. Virtually all computer software is governed as much by license as by fair use. Once you accept the license that comes with the software, whatever that license says is what you must do. If you agree to something less than fair use, you are bound to that. If the license grants you broader rights than fair use would otherwise give you, you may take advantage of that, too. As far as other teachers using the clip art, if the license is for the school, they would be bound by that license as well.

Fair Use | Cover Art on the Web

? *I would like to add a "Book of the Month" feature to our school's Web site, where I give a short summary of the book, title, and author. I would like to scan a picture of the book cover and post it to go with the summary so parents and students can have a visual. Is this violating copyright law, or is it okay to do this since it is for educational purposes, and I give credit by posting both author and publisher?*

© Just giving credit isn't really enough. And the author of the book probably didn't do that art on the cover (some picture books are an exception), so crediting the author isn't appropriate either. If your image were only available to your students, you could claim educational purposes under the TEACH Act, but it isn't. It is available to the entire world via the Web. So here is the analysis:

- **Use:** nonprofit, but not educational (since it isn't for a class) and not criticism or commentary since it is just stuck up there (you aren't talking about the art, in other words).
- **Nature:** creative, but published
- **Amount:** ALL of it (never a good thing)
- **Effect of use on value of work:** unknown since creator hasn't been consulted. He may have plans to use the image for posters, or bookmarks, or his own Web site, and your use dilutes his own use.

It is a calculated risk. Go to the publisher's Web site. Sometimes they have files there for download for just such purposes, and they grant permission to use them. If you don't find that, I would request permission.

Fair Use | *Creating a Derivative Work*

? *We have a new high tech graphic arts lab in which students scan images (paintings, photos) and use image-editing software to transform them into something entirely different. What are the copyright issues with this? The transformed image is not recognizable as what it was.*

© The issues you describe are common but not clearly defined in copyright law. You describe a process of making a copy (scanning) and creating a derivative work. Both of these are rights reserved for the copyright owner. Now, a student can make a single copy of an image for his or her personal use under fair use. The problem is the alteration and creation of a digital work. If the student gets the base image from the Internet or an electronic source, there is a significant possibility that the work has a digital watermark, an invisible copyright tag embedded in the file, which will make it a simple matter for someone to discover that the work has been copied and altered. So, if the student makes a copy and uses it only for class work and *keeps the product*, there should be no problem. You are on much shakier ground if the student displays the art, mounts it on a Web site, or makes other public use of it.

Fair Use | Displaying Book Covers

? *Is it against copyright law to display the original cover of a book as a separate entity? For example, what about a book that is withdrawn due to damage but some of the covers and the pages are still salvageable? I will be using these for display purposes only, not for regular face-to-face instruction.*

© Your proposed use is certainly fair. You own the paper on which the cover is printed, and if you choose to discard the rest of the book and retain the cover (or some modification of that plan) you can certainly do that. You can't mount a scan of the cover on the Web, or make a derivative work, or do other intellectual things with the cover without permission for non-instructional uses, but just keeping the image and enjoying it is certainly within the doctrine of "first sale" that ends the copyright owner's right of distribution on that single copy of the work.

Fair Use | Fair Use and Pictures on the Web

? *I have been allowing my students to copy and paste pictures from the Web into their documents as long as they cite that they did so. Is this a violation of copyright laws or does it fall into the fair use category?*

© Check the section on the multimedia fair use guidelines in *Copyright for Schools: A Practical Guide, 4th Edition* (Linworth Publishing, Inc., 2005), or any other standard copyright reference work. As long as the use is for a multimedia project, students are bound by these rules. If you are using the images in a word-processing document, students may make use of copies of images following the print guidelines. (Since there are no Internet rules at this moment, we must fall back on the rules we have.) One caveat: The student may use a single copy of a picture (with citation, of course) in a paper under fair use, but the paper must revert to the student. It can't be published or displayed except live in the class for which it was created. The student (more properly the student's parents) can give permission for publication or display to happen to the student's part of the work, but the student doesn't own the images and hence can't give permission for those to be republished or displayed. Those rights remain with the copyright holder. Standard fair use rules apply to non-educational uses such as publication or Web display.

Fair Use | Images of Public Art

? *I would like to add some images of public art to our Web site. These objects are all in areas that are either outdoors or inside but in a public space. Do we need to get permission from the original work's copyright holder?*

© If you had asked about architecture, the answer would be easy. In the United States, section 120(a) of the copyright law tells us that the copyright in a work of architecture "does not include the right to prevent the making, distributing, or public display of pictures, paintings, photographs, or other pictorial representations of the work, if the building in which the work is embodied is located in or ordinarily visible from a public place." With outdoor sculpture or paintings, the answer isn't as clear.

You would own the copyright in the photograph itself, but the photograph of a two-dimensional work of art might not be original enough to qualify for a copyright. Remember that anything published before 1923 is in the public domain in the United States, and may be freely copied. For anything published before 1964, if the copyright was not renewed the work is in the public domain. After that, renewal was automatic. If the work you wish to feature is still under copyright, you can expect that the original artist(s) might object.

Fair Use | Making Copies of Images

? *I would like to take from the Internet reproductions of book covers of the books on this year's state book award list and combine them in a collage that I could insert in a "create-it-yourself" mug from a local coffee store. My kids see me carry my mugs around and I feel that this would help to generate interest in the state book award program. I would like to also make a couple of these mugs to donate to the scholarship auction for our state media conference. Would this be possible?*

© Making a copy of the images for your own personal use is fair. But when you start distributing the images, and with an exchange of money involved, (and with publishers there to see it!) you are getting on the very ragged edge. I wouldn't think this would be a fair use. Of course, you can always ask for permission. The publishers might agree since this promotes their material and the proceeds benefit the media association that is honoring their books.

Fair Use | Newspaper Pictures

? *We would like to do a visual display for Black History Month. We copied several pictures out of various books, but all of the pictures are actually part of old newspaper articles on slavery. Are we in violation of copyright by using these copied newspaper pictures from books for our display?*

© A teacher can make a single copy of something from a book and use that copy in teaching. The copy may be retained (and used) from year to year. See the print copy guidelines in my book, *Copyright for Schools: A Practical Guide, 4th Edition* (Linworth Publishing, Inc., 2005), or any other copyright book for details of the print guidelines. If those pictures were made before 1923, they're no longer protected by copyright anyway, so it's important to locate the true source of the images.

Fair Use | *PowerPoint Picture Books*

? *One of our library technicians made a PowerPoint by scanning all of the pictures in a book. She shows the PowerPoint as she reads the book. She is using it the way we more mature folks used to use an opaque projector, when we put the whole book under the lens so that everyone could see it. Because she is scanning the entire book, is this an abuse of copyright? Or, is it okay since she is giving proper attribution to the author and the illustrator because she is introducing, reading, and then discussing the book itself, and just using the PowerPoint presentation to enrich the lesson?*

© Copyright wise, she is copying the entire work. There are very few "fair uses" that would allow making a copy of an entire work. Per the multimedia guidelines, she can copy five images from a book, but I doubt that would cover a picture book. I'd recommend using a document camera instead. You are projecting the item, but the display is ephemeral—it isn't saved and stored. Showing a book during storytime is a protected use. No worries there. It is the copying and saving that is the problem.

Fair Use | Reproducing Images in Newsletters

? *Our library newsletter includes images of book jackets obtained from online booksellers. We only use images that do not have a copyright statement. We were told that, if there was no copyright statement, we can use such images. I've read that copyright law protects works even if a copyright notice is not provided. So, is this illegal and should we stop this practice? Also, if a library subscribes to a service that provides images, book jackets, and so forth with their automation system for public display on their catalog or their Web site, can the library also use the images to reproduce them in print?*

© You are correct. No copyright notice has been required since 1976. One must always assume that any document or image, unless you know positively to the contrary, is protected by copyright. One might make a case of fair use of these images, using the four tests of fair use. If the image is a work in itself, however, using the image may not be fair. If it is an image that is part of a whole, the entire fair use assessment would come into play. Because these images are not being used to teach content in a class, none of the educational exemptions would apply here. Regarding the subscription images, the answer would be to look in the license or subscription agreement. That will define what permissions the library has regarding re-purposing of the images from the service.

Fair Use | Web Page Images

? *One of our teachers is creating a Web page for the school and would like to use a single graphic from the National Geographic Web site. We're concerned that the "all rights reserved" at the top of the pages means we can't use the desired graphic from that page. If we use it, are we committing copyright infringement?*

© The image is protected by copyright. Unless you have permission, you don't want to re-use the image on a Web page, primarily because you're using the entire image. Your usage would be nonprofit, but not directly related to education, and you're distributing the image to the world on the Internet. Using the single image in a PowerPoint presentation probably would be possible per the multimedia guidelines, but those are specific to that medium. Your intended Web page use proposes to copy and distribute, not a probable fair use situation, especially as it doesn't involve direct teaching.

Fair Use | Web Pictures

? *A teacher wants to use a few Web pictures of the Mayan civilization in a paper for her graduate class. Is citing the source enough? This paper will not be published and will be returned to her.*

© Citation is probably sufficient in this case, as long as not more than a few images come from a single source. Under the print guidelines a teacher or student can make a single copy of a graphic for personal use, including teaching. The copies may be retained. Further use of the images (Web publication) would require additional permission. While Web sites aren't technically "print," the images will be printed for use in the paper. Even going back to the baseline fair use guidelines will provide a positive outcome for this question because the use is nonprofit and transformative.

Public Display | Book Character Murals

? *Some teachers would like to have book characters painted on the walls of our school to promote reading. I feel this is in violation of copyright law, but have not found specific information to give them.*

© This use is likely NOT fair. The characters are not only protected by copyright they are trademarked, and there is no fair use of trademark. It is always a good idea to ask the artist who paints a mural to present verification of clearance of the characters. Of course, he can always paint fairy tale or folktale characters if he creates his own rendition of them and doesn't copy the works of illustrators such as Steven Kellogg, etc.

Public Display | Cartoon Images

? *Our PTA wants to paint cartoon/storybook figures on the walls in our school. Is this permitted?*

© The artist, publishing company, or production company owns the copyright to the images in books and cartoons. Even copied images that are not exact duplicates are still considered copies. I like to use the "If it looks like it, it is" rule of thumb. So if your mural has an image that can be identified as Snoopy®—even if the image isn't an exact duplicate of one drawn by Charles Shultz—it is an image of Snoopy® as far as the law is concerned. Take this situation through the four tests of fair use:

1. You are a nonprofit educational organization (a point in your favor).

2. The material being copied is creative, not factual (a point against you).

3. The amount of material being copied is substantial—you are copying the whole character rather than a hand or an eye (a point against you).

4. The purpose of your copying the character is to avoid buying legitimate, licensed art (a significant point against you).

So you see by this analysis, you have three points against you, one of which is significant by itself. Only one of the tests of fair use is in your favor, and that point alone isn't enough to justify a claim of fair use. Some production companies have been reported to arrive at schools and demand that infringing murals be painted over on the spot. Be careful.

Public Display | Displaying Book Covers on the Web

? *Can I scan book covers and post them to my Web site with student reviews? The LM_Net archives illuminate the conflicting point of view regarding this issue. My instructor for my Web Design class said he thought it was within fair use guidelines. What's your opinion?*

© You have the fair use right to make a copy of ONE graphic from a book and retain that graphic for use in teaching. HOWEVER, redistributing that graphic to the world is NOT a fair use right. There are companies (Syndetic Solutions, for example) that SELL rights to book covers in electronic format for such uses. Remember that a fundamental principle of fair use is that you must not be taking money out of someone's pocket. If there is licensing available, you must have some REALLY private uses to get around the requirement to pay. Here, this is far from a private use (on the Web is distribution to the world) and there is licensing available. Some publishers may not care, others do. But you don't get to make that decision.

Some may argue that the use is transformative in that the reviews are criticism or commentary, but the review isn't of the book cover, it is of the content of the book. It's a judgment call here. Now that publishers can make a little money from the book cover images, they may be less likely to turn the other cheek regarding use. Depending on how risk averse you are, you may just want to license the images.

Public Display | Displaying Cartoons

? *A teacher has plastered his walls with newspaper cartoons. Is it a copyright violation for teachers to cut out cartoons and display them?*

© Presuming that the teacher bought the book or newspaper, she may cut it up and post the cartoons on her wall. The teacher may also make a single copy of a cartoon for her personal use or for teaching. Beware of assembling the cartoons into an anthology, however. Making an anthology is not allowed under fair use.

Public Display | *Graphics and Music Manuscripts*

? *A class in our high school is creating an exposé type of book of their own original creative writing and artwork. These books will be distributed and advertisements sold to cover the cost. However, they have designed a cover that includes black and white copies of famous artwork and music manuscripts. There are two da Vinci's, two Van Gogh's, the* Nutcracker Suite *music, and two of Mozart's music. These black and white images will wrap around to the back and will be in color on the back. Are these famous pieces of work, because of their age, in the public domain and can therefore be used?*

© The artwork should be fine. Van Gogh, the most contemporary, died in 1890. Even applying today's copyright term the work would be in the public domain after 1960. Mozart, if not a post-1923 arrangement, would be public domain. Tchaikovsky died in 1893. Remember that new arrangements get new copyrights, so always check to see that the arrangement being used is pre-1923 or the original if you want to be certain you are dealing with public domain materials.

Public Display | *Graphics Over Channel One*

? We do the school announcements over the Channel One broadcast system, using PowerPoint and an Aver Key to interface with the Channel One system. The announcements are silent because the faculty members like to be able to turn their TV on whenever they are ready for the students to view the announcements. Sometimes I announce new books in the library, but I have never attempted to include any pictures or graphics, as I am not sure just what the copyright restrictions are in this situation. Could you advise me?

© It is certainly within fair use to put up a copy of an image of a book within or near your library for teaching purposes. It is also fair use to hold up the copy live to booktalk, read, etc. The further afield you get from those two protected uses, the more risk you assume. These are your students but they are not in your class. You are distributing, but the use is transformative and you are using a very small part of the book. As long as this broadcast doesn't leave the building (as opposed to putting things on a Web page that is distributed to the world) you are probably pretty safe.

Public Display | *Home Use Only Video*

? *In checking some videos I noticed this warning: "This videocassette contains copyrighted programs and is licensed for PRIVATE HOME USE ONLY. Public performance of any kind, including, but not limited to, school and library showings, is strictly prohibited."*

I have never seen a warning that specifically mentioned it could not be shown in a school setting. I guess we need to get rid of it, but before I do that I was wondering if others have seen this on videos in their collection.

© If you are using this program for DIRECT INSTRUCTION (in other words, meeting the five tests of AV fair use) you don't need public performance rights (PPR). You are exempt from the PPR requirements in that instance. The notice you see is the "home use only" warning that is on so many videos. All it would appear to mean is that there are no public performance rights on that copy of the tape. But if you are doing DIRECT TEACHING on that topic, and meet the other requirements of AV fair use, you don't need public performance rights.

Understand, however, that if this video was shrink-wrapped, or was purchased under some express or implied license, you may have waived your fair use rights by accepting the license.

Chapter Three: Graphic Materials **79**

Public Display | *Photocopy Pictures for Bulletin Boards*

? *Photocopied pictures of scenes from movies are displayed on a bulletin board. Some pictures are from old movies while others are more recent. I didn't select the pictures, so I am not sure if more than one came from the same book. Is this a violation?*

© If the bulletin board uses the teacher's own copies of these photos, there should be no problem. Remember that under fair use, anyone may make a single copy of something like a photo or chart for his personal research or teaching.

Public Display | *Photographs of Paintings*

? *I am putting up a Web page and want to post images of Cézanne's and Van Gogh's paintings. If I take a photograph of a painting, can I use this?*

© If you can get the museum to allow you to take a photo of the original (which is long out of copyright) you can post it. But if you scan a professional photo of the old master painting, you have violated the copyright of the photographer (or more likely the museum which owns the painting since they probably commissioned the photos). The reason museums don't allow photos isn't so much that the flash damages the paintings but because they get big bucks from selling reproductions of the paintings! However, a photograph of a painting that contains nothing but the painting itself, with no or minimal creativity in the positioning of the camera or the lighting, no copyright will apply to the photograph and you may use the work despite any purported copyright notice on the work. The photographer cannot get a copyright on a slavish reproduction of an original (and a direct copy of a painting would fit that definition).

Public Display | Student Copies Church Painting

? *A teacher wants to enter a student painting in a contest. The student painted a copy of a picture that hangs in his church. Has the student violated copyright law? What about all those "take-offs" from the* American Gothic *painting that have been done?*

© Assuming the painting in the church was created after 1923, the student didn't violate copyright, but did employ fair use to make a copy of a work for his personal research and education. The problem arises when the painting is exhibited publicly. The student can use the copy for the class, but doing a public exhibition is another problem altogether. The work may still be protected by copyright, hence would be restricted from copying beyond educational fair use. The *American Gothic* painting (created in 1930) may be in the public domain now, so take-offs wouldn't be an issue in that case. Parodies of works (where for which the derivative work is poking fun at the original) are protected "speech," per many court rulings.

Public Display | *Taking Graphics from the Internet*

? *In our Communication Graphics class, students have created calendars and other items such as advertisements, posters, etc. for class assignments. The emphasis is on visual attraction with few words. Each student is allowed to select the images or graphics they want to use to fulfill the assignment. Most often these images come off the Internet. Graphics, etc. were not from royalty free or public domain sites. The department wants to display our students' work at a Career and Technology Education Exhibit at a local mall. Any problems with this?*

© Students can use those graphics for personal use and education, including display within/near the classroom with no issues. Once you remove the display to a very public place like a mall, all bets are off. You can go through the traditional fair use assessment graphic by graphic to determine if the use of each piece meets fair use, and that would be necessary for such a public display. Some of those images might also be trademarks, and trademarks have different considerations than copyright. There is no fair use for trademarks.

Chapter Three: Graphic Materials 83

Public Display | Using Book Characters for Murals

? Our art teacher would like to have her elementary students paint a mural in the library combining characters from children's literature. These would not be a direct copy from a book, but rather a combination of characters within an original setting. None of the characters would be Disney, but rather from artists such as Tomie de Paola, etc. This would be an educational effort, to teach art skills. There would be no financial gain to this. Is it okay?

© No, financial gain isn't the big consideration here. Note that many artists are just as aggressive about protecting characters as Disney, Shel Silverstein, etc., are. What you are doing is creating a derivative work. Students have the right to do this for their own education (art skills), but the copies must vest with the student. You are planning to do a daily public display of these characters, and the daily display has nothing to do with coursework. The copies will not be with the students, rather they will stay at the school, and the purpose is to avoid paying for licensed copies of artwork. None of these is a reason in your favor.

I wouldn't recommend this project to you. As an alternative idea, the students can read several versions of a tale (Cinderella, for example) and then draw their own versions of the characters. However, remember that the students own the copyrights to their own work, and you will want signed releases from the students' parents (because the students are minors) to retain and display the work. I would probably recommend that you request all rights to the work so that at some point in the future you can decide to paint over the mural, thereby destroying it. Ask a copyright attorney to look over the agreement.

Chapter Four

Sound Recordings and Music

Sound recordings are not the same as music, despite what logic might tell you. Music is generally a printed work—notes written on staff paper—but it can be any form of musical notation registered in any standard format such as a computer file or other musical archival system. A sound recording can include music, but it can just as easily be a recording of spoken words, or birdcalls, or heartbeats. The recordings must be saved in some tangible form such as grooves in a vinyl disc, iron filings on magnetic tape, or laser etchings on special types of plastic, as well as zeros and ones on a computer disc. All qualify as sound recordings.

Copyright owners weren't too concerned about copies of sound recordings until digital technologies appeared on the scene. Before digital recordings, making copies of records or audiotapes was not a very successful process, even with multiple duplicating equipment. Second generation recordings degraded to the point that even lay people could detect the decline of quality. With the advent of digital recordings (CDs), each copy is as perfect as the original. An additional problem is that digital recording formats such as MP3 are native to computers, which makes transfer of digital files a fast, easy, and perfect process via the

Internet. Once file sharing of sound recordings was perfected, millions of copies of copyrighted sound recordings criss-crossed the Internet daily. Record companies' revenues plummeted as consumers found that free copies of desired sound recordings were just as good as the ones they had to pay close to $20 for in the record stores. Record companies scrambled to find ways to protect their investment in products.

Record companies aren't the only ones who lose with pirated recordings. In the case of recorded music, some artist wrote the music that was performed and recorded. Turning to look at the written side of the recording industry, thousands of songwriters, well known and unknown, make their livings from royalties on sales of recorded versions of their works. In addition, the performing side of the triangle asserts that each performance is unique; therefore they deserve a return on their investment in the performance made permanent in the recording. They receive a piece of the royalty pie on each sale, too. Every file transferred without payment takes money not only from the recording conglomerates but also from the composers who create the songs and the artists who perform them. In self-defense, the record companies and artists/composers have formed industry associations whose primary purpose is to track down and punish those miscreants who distribute copies of sound recordings without permission or royalty payment. Groups such as the Recording Industry Artists' Association (RIAA); The American Society of Composers, Authors and Publishers (ASCAP); Broadcast Music, Inc. (BMI); and (SESAC) vigorously track down recordings pirates and litigate against the offenders.

Schools' primary concern with the use of sound recordings is public performance. Any performance (playing) of a sound recording in a school would be a public performance since school is a public place (outside a home and family). However, performances of sound recordings would qualify for a fair use exemption in the same manner as playing a video would qualify as a fair use if the performance were for students and teachers in a class, the school is a nonprofit educational organization, the showing takes place in a classroom or other instructional place, the recording being used is legally acquired, and if the recording is being used for direct teaching. Entertainment, reward, or other non-instructional performances would not automatically qualify for an educational exemption and would necessitate a four-factor review.

Printed music has its own set of guidelines for use in schools. For the most part, music companies are worried that schools will purchase one copy of sheet music and then duplicate the needed copies rather than purchase them. An entire set of music guidelines are mounted on the Music Library Association Web site, and they are explained in *Copyright for Schools: A Practical Guide*, *4th Edition* (Linworth Publishing, Inc., 2005), or any other comprehensive work on copyright law.

Generally | *Archival Copies of Audiotapes*

? *One of our teachers has purchased an audiotape of a class book that she wants to loan to a student to listen to at home. However, she's concerned about the tape possibly getting lost or damaged. Can she make a copy to send home with the student?*

© Making backup copies of personally owned media for personal use **at home** is fine. For example, if you purchased a tape for yourself, and want to transfer the tape to your MP3 player to listen to, that is fine. However, as a school you do not have the legal ability to create archival copies of materials that are not *in an obsolete format* or are not *damaged and unable to be replaced at a reasonable price*. Media producers sometimes offer archival rights (the authority to make backup copies) with their materials, or sell that at a slight fee. You would need to contact the producer of the tape in question to see if they offer those rights for sale. Also note that there is a significant difference in what the general public is allowed to do in the privacy of their own homes (taping and retaining television programs, for example) and what personnel at school are allowed to do in classrooms and libraries. It is essential that you separate those two locations when calculating copyright repercussions.

Generally | Archiving Books on CD

? *May books on CD be archived if the copy is never, ever circulated at the same time as the original? I think that if it is for a school library AND K-6 these factors make a difference.*

© The only medium that may be backed up or archived is computer software. That term would include CD-ROMs, but not audio CDs. The grade level and the fact that the library is in a school are not mitigating circumstances.

Generally | Band Music

? *Our school purchases all of our band music for each piece (1st trumpets, a copy for everyone; 3rd trumpet, a copy for everyone; oboe, a copy for each; etc.). But because students lose and/or mutilate their music, the band director files the original, purchased pieces and makes a copy for each student. This way, if the tuba player loses his piece, the entire band doesn't suffer. Is this a violation, since our intent is NOT to keep the copyright holder from any due profits?*

© An interesting question, and an odd use. Technically he is making an "archival" copy of the music, which isn't permitted. Only in certain preservation situations is making copies of print materials okay, and this use doesn't qualify in that case. If new copies of the music are still available at a "reasonable price" (such as the original price, not some artificially inflated price), then the band director is obligated to purchase replacement copies. So in this case, the band director is depriving the copyright holder of sales.

Generally | Citing Music Sources

? *If we were to use short bits of music from CDs we own in a daily announcement program, would we be required to cite resources and use a copyright disclaimer at the beginning as we do in a multimedia project?*

© Anytime you use anything that you didn't create you have an ethical obligation to cite the source. How can you expect students to cite their sources if you aren't doing it? A copyright attorney once told me that if you don't cite your source, it is ALWAYS a copyright violation, no matter how little you use or where you use it.

Generally | *Fair Use of Downloaded Music*

? *Does classroom use of downloaded music from the Internet fit under "fair use" if the teacher is using it within a lesson? One of our teachers uses it as background music when he is not teaching. I also suspect that he is using music brought in by students who have done the downloading. I would appreciate some wording I can use to inform students and teachers as to what is "fair use" of Internet music and what is not.*

© I would suggest you apply the AV fair use guidelines to any analysis of classroom use of ANY type of audiovisual. You must answer YES to all five questions below in order to qualify as fair use:

1. Are you a nonprofit educational institution?

2. Is the performance by and for (only) students and teachers in a regular class?

3. Does the performance take place in a classroom or other instructional place?

4. Is the performance made from a legal copy of the work? (Your downloaded music isn't going to qualify here unless you have purchased it from iTunes™ or similar sites.)

5. Is the performance directly related to the lesson at hand? (This works for the music teacher who is teaching about a work, or a history teacher playing period music, but not for motivational or background music.)

Of course, whatever music you have that is licensed for public performance (royalty-free CDs for example) is usable in whatever way is stated on your license.

Generally | Mechanical Reproduction Rights of Musicals

? *Our district wants to air school plays or musicals on local cable access. I understand that the school would need to obtain mechanical reproduction rights to videotape the presentation for any reason other than critique by the performing students and teachers. How does a school obtain mechanical reproduction rights, and is there an expense with that? Are there other copyright clearances that are needed? This one broadcast would probably only be seen by family and friends of the students, so the use shouldn't be a big deal. I believe cable access of such presentations would not fit under the guidelines for distance learning.*

© The mechanical license is available from the same company that sold the rights to the play. You are correct that the airing of the play on cable does not fit the distance learning guidelines (which haven't been approved yet anyway). Whether you think that cable use is insignificant or not makes no difference. It is up to the copyright owner to make those determinations. Perhaps they will agree with you and allow you to do the showing gratis, but since this is their livelihood it is doubtful. You are in better negotiating position to make broadcast arrangements *before* you have contracted for the play, stating that the company that provides the best package deal will get your business. Once you have contracted for the copies of the play, the company has the control: either you pay their stipulated fee or you don't get to record and broadcast the performance.

Generally | Online Music for Video

? *Have you heard of any school subscribing to music sites like Napster™ or iTunes™ to download copyrighted MP3s and use for in house video production? I can't find education-specific information on their sites.*

© While schools certainly could subscribe to those sites, I'm quite sure that the rights they get when they pay to download music don't include the necessary synch or mechanical rights needed for video production. I doubt the sites have even considered educational uses of the music there. Remember, those sites are only royalty collectors for the copyright owners: the sites do not own and cannot license the music for any other reason than personal use on a music device. For the types of uses you suggest you need to contact the Harry Fox Agency. Of course, under the multimedia guidelines there is the 30-second limit for music in PowerPoint and similar productions when following the rest of the guidelines. A legally licensed copy of digital music could be used for those purposes. So if you need a clip of a song and you don't own the CD, paying 99 cents to download the song from an online site is less expensive than paying $20 to purchase the CD to get a legal copy of the song to use in your multimedia production. You might also try clip music sites such as <www.freeplaymusic.com> that offer limited uses for educational applications at no cost.

Generally | Replacing Damaged Audio Recording

? *Today I tried to order another set of* To Kill a Mockingbird *on CD or cassette and was told it is out-of-print from all the publishers. It's true. I have looked on most of the audio vendor Web sites: Recorded Books, Books on Tape, etc. If we only have one copy, is it okay to make an archive copy and circulate the copied set?*

© Is something wrong with the set? You can make a repair copy, but you can't make an "in case" copy. It works like this. You can make REPAIR copies if "an unused replacement is unavailable at a reasonable price." In other words, if yours breaks, you can make a copy to replace it if you can't BUY one at that time. But you can't start making additional copies (or archive copies) just because the work is out-of-print. Doing that removes the economic incentive from publishers to republish it.

Generally | Selling Copies of Videotaped Music Performance

? *Our music director would like to sell copies of a videotaped performance of the school musical to students and parents. Is this a copyright violation?*

© Most likely. A school may make a single tape of a performance of a copyrighted work, but only for the purpose of evaluating student performance. The copy may not be duplicated, distributed, or sold. Of course, if the rights to make and sell copies were purchased with the music or playbook, the music director may make whatever copies such license details.

Generally | Using a Song on CCT

? *The morning news program that we broadcast to classrooms on a closed circuit television network uses a song from a movie as its theme song. The song is not changed in any way. Is this fair use?*

© Because this isn't part of face-to-face instruction, you should go through a four-test fair use analysis to determine if your limited use is fair. Remember that as part of an assessment of fair use you must consider:

1. **Brevity** - How much of the song do you use? (If you use all of the song, you are at more risk than if you just use a single phrase.)

2. **Spontaneity** - Do you have time to get permissions? (If you have been using the same song for more than two weeks, you have had time.)

I would say that you passed the boundaries of fair use after you used the song for two weeks.

In Class | Helping Students with Low Reading Ability

? One of our teachers would like to make an audio copy of individual chapters in her social studies textbook for several students who have extremely low reading ability. She would like to download it onto the laptops of the students who need it. I'm not sure if they qualify as special education or not. Is this permissible? Would she be able to keep this recording indefinitely? What would the teacher have to do to help these students who cannot read the textbook? It's becoming increasingly frustrating to have the technology to do these kinds of things for students yet not be able to help them.

© No, this use is not permissible under fair use. She has the ability to make a copy of ONE chapter, but not multiple chapters. There is a special exception for students who are unable to use standard print, but it wouldn't appear that these students qualify for that exception. In addition, the exception specifies that the format must be in Braille or the "Recording for the Blind" 4-track cassette format that isn't playable on standard cassette players. Kurzweil files are also acceptable. There is no provision for computer playback.

I understand your frustration, but the law hasn't caught up to the technology yet. Your options right now are to request permission from the publisher (who is very likely to give it since you did buy the books) or to contact your Congressional representative and hope for a change in the law (which is very UNlikely considering the pro-business stance that this Congress has adopted.)

In Class | Making Band Music Available via Password

? *Our band teacher purchased music to use with the band. The music comes with a CD of the song(s) being performed. Can he put the songs up on the Internet for students to access if he uses a password?*

© This is a TEACH Act question. If he is going to be using the song to teach students (direct instruction, not just enrichment or extra-curricular activities) and this is a one-time use (he isn't going to use this CD every semester from now on) this use would likely be okay. The fact that he is using the whole song may be a bit more problematic, but the limited term of use and the restricted access via password are points in his favor. TEACH recommends not using complete or long works, but this song wouldn't be long, so I think you are probably okay here for a single song. The more he uses that CD, the poorer his fair use defenses would be.

In Class | Music in Student Productions

? *Can a communications class, in which the teacher is teaching students to prepare a news program, download music from the Internet to use in student productions?*

© This appears to be face-to-face instruction. If you keep the results within the classroom, and if the music you download is legal, you are within a standard fair use analysis. However, if the downloaded music is protected by copyright, and is downloaded from a file sharing service, the copy isn't legal and you would not be within fair use. The wider the resulting program is displayed, the less likely the use would be fair.

In Class | Music Performance

? *Our language arts teacher requested music from other cultures to incorporate into her lessons. What's the copyright rule if she's playing it only for educational purposes? Does that constitute "fair use"?*

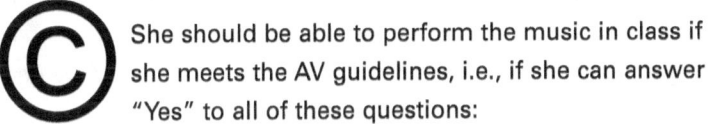

She should be able to perform the music in class if she meets the AV guidelines, i.e., if she can answer "Yes" to all of these questions:

1. Nonprofit educational institution,
2. Performance in classroom or other instructional place,
3. Performance by and for students and teachers in the class,
4. Performance directly related to the lesson at hand, and
5. Performance of a legally acquired copy of the work.

If you answer "No" to any of these questions, the use is considered to be a public performance, and you must obtain permission or pay royalties.

In Class | Public Domain Songs

? A student asked, *"I want to be able to send out my next productions to festivals and competitions, but I still want music in them. The best way to do that would be to use classical/public domain songs. One that I already have in mind is* Shenandoah, *the civil war song. It plays at the end of* Nixon *and they credit it as traditional, but they also say it is courtesy of London Records. I just want to know my boundaries. Is there a way I can find out what's traditional and what's not? Or at least, what is the easiest way to do that?"*

© Sound recordings are protected just like new works, so anything recorded after 1972 is protected in the U.S. The underlying composition may be in the public domain (so that is one less clearance hurdle you must get) but the recording of that public domain song still is protected by the performance copyright. The ideal thing is to use a service called Public Domain Reports. They have HUGE lists of public domain music, and will sell you the sheet music. Then you use a computer to perform the music (or perform it yourself on some instrument or *a capella*). As an option, you can use some of the royalty free discs or online services. A lot of those are downloadable by track for not much money, and you can use the songs in any way other than re-selling the music for clips without paying additional fees. The <www.freeplaymusic.com> Web site offers inexpensive or free (depending on use) music in varying length clips. They have an extensive library from which to choose.

Public Performance | Audio CDs for Workshops

? *It is common practice in my district to do a PowerPoint presentation for the school board showing aspects of various programs. Nearly all use an audio CD and play entire songs with their presentation. Based on your book (1st edition) it would appear that to play the entire song to staff one would need permission. Do we need a new edition of your book?*

© Yes, you do need to get the new (4th) edition because, based on recent changes, the 1st edition has a lot of inaccurate information. Check out the multimedia fair use guidelines at <http://www.utsystem.edu/OGC/IntellectualProperty/ccmcguid.htm>. They give limited permission to use audio, however, they are only for face-to-face instruction. The school board meeting doesn't qualify, but a workshop would. Consider purchasing some royalty free music CDs (Soundzabound has a three CD set for $99) that can be used in such circumstances, or investigate <www.freeplaymusic.com>.

Public Performance | *Broadcasting a Musical Program*

? *Our music teacher produces a musical every other year with interested students. She has had trouble getting copyright approval for a local cable company to broadcast our productions and for parents or the school to videotape. We wondered if copyright would be an issue if we produced a musical revue instead. This would bring in the 10% rule. Her plan is to purchase sheet music (and words) as needed for each student and to then choose one musical number from each of a collection of musicals rather than performing one entire musical.*

© Well, to begin with, there is no such thing as a "10% rule." You either meet the various educational guidelines for use of specific materials or the baseline fair use guidelines, or you don't. The problem with your plan to perform one song each from various musicals is that each of the songs of a musical bears its own copyright. The musical is an anthology of songs accompanying a play, not a single work. So when you do a fair use analysis of this, you come out on the short end. Using such pieces in a classroom setting would be fine, but to broadcast the material on cable and make multiple tapes would be the sticking points again. Here is how it shakes out:

- Purpose and character of the use: You are nonprofit educational, but the cable company isn't. You lose on this one. Your use isn't for criticism or commentary, either.
- Nature of the copyrighted work: These are highly creative and therefore more strictly protected. You lose on this one.
- The amount of the work used: You would use the entire song. You lose on this one.
- The effect of your use on the market for or value of the work: Because cable is for-profit and people must pay to access the work, you have lost on this one, too.

It just doesn't look good at all for your proposed use. Your best bet is to license or get permission. To license, contact ASCAP or BMI. They have online databases of songs, so you can find out what the rights would cost and who owns the copyrights. Note that live performance, in a school, for which no admission is charged would be a fair use under the Music guidelines.

Public Performance | *Broadcasting School Music*

? *We would like to broadcast school music programs on our local cable channel. The broadcasts would include school choir, orchestra, and band concerts over the public access channels of our local cable company. Does cable broadcast go beyond educational fair use? I think showing the same tape in school to students is appropriate because they learn by reviewing their performance.*

© What you describe regarding the cable channel is a public performance, and it will require a broadcast license to be used in the manner you describe. Contact ASCAP (The American Society of Composers, Authors and Publishers) or BMI (Broadcast Music, Inc.) for the fees required. Permitted taping rules allow ONE copy of a performance to be made, and that performance is restricted to use in the classroom ONLY for critique by the performers and their director.

Public Performance | Choir Caroling

? *If our school choir goes caroling, is it a public performance? They go door-to-door, singing inside people's homes (or in their doorways), or on the street. If the carolers receive cookies and cocoa, is it a performance for profit? What if the choir performs in a shopping mall while strolling within its space?*

© If the carolers sing inside private homes or on doorsteps, a case might be made for a non-public performance. If the performance is public, you might rely on fair use (section 107). Also, look at the exemption under section 110(4). If the performance is in the street, then there's no admission charge, even if the performers receive some compensation. For the performance in the shopping mall, ASCAP or BMI might license the mall for performances of background music. Such a license would cover the choir's performance.

Public Performance | Downloaded Music

? *In a daily announcements program broadcast to the entire school, may we use music clips downloaded from the Internet?*

© One of the important factors in a fair use analysis is a legal copy of the work being used. There are a lot of sites on the Internet where you can download free music, but there are just as many pirate sites. Make sure that you are using a legal copy of whatever music you use. But there is still a lot of missing information in your question. Are the music and the performance in the public domain? How much are you using? All that information feeds into this analysis.

Public Performance | Internet Radio

? *I have found several radio stations that do streaming audio. If a teacher wanted background music could she play this through her computer to the class?*

© Not without a license. There are some cases where businesses tried that to avoid paying for Muzak by playing the radio in the store for the benefit of the customers. They lost. If the purpose is to set an atmosphere for the class, the benefit is public and the performance is not exempt. Playing just for the personal benefit of the teacher, however, is okay. Of course, if there is a LITTLE spillover that is understandable, but playing at a volume sufficient to be heard in the entire classroom would be no doubt a public performance. Naturally, any direct classroom instruction using music would meet the educational exemption.

Public Performance | Music in Multimedia

? *A teacher has students create commercials using music that has been downloaded from the Internet. He wants to know if it is legal to use the music in their commercials. I told him that it wouldn't be if it had been downloaded from a pirate site. Using your book, I was also able to tell him about the 30-second limit, and that he wouldn't be able to show it on our local cable station (because students in the class are the only ones allowed to view the copyrighted material.) Did I advise him correctly?*

© Thirty seconds is the max limit for music that is more than 300 SECONDS long. For works less than 300 seconds (five minutes) you can only use 10%. The guidelines state that the student's use must be only for class or personal use (showing it to Grandma, etc.) so cable distribution would probably not be a good plan. The entire use is predicated on a legally acquired copy of the work being used. If the student and teacher are sure the site is pirated, it would be a bad thing to use anything from the site (and a horrible example to set). But if they pay for the music (like iTunes™), the copy would be legal and would be okay. You might encourage them to look at some of the free clip music sites like <www.freeplaymusic.com>.

Public Performance | Music Recording Performance

? *A teacher is presenting at a conference and she has created movement to go with songs. She is taking the legally purchased CD and playing it on a boom box. She is not copying anything. She is not being paid anything. If anything, she could be helping sell the CDs. I know fair use covers classroom use and not staff development. I know for movies, the above circumstance would be considered public performance. What about music?*

© Yes, this is certainly public performance. Possible good news: depending on where she is doing the performance, the hall may have a venue license that covers such performances. She needs to ask. Failing that, a four-factor, fair use analysis would be in order.

Public Performance | *Playing Classical Music for Inspiration*

? *Can a teacher play a CD or tape of classical music in the classroom as inspiration to students during writing time? All of the brain-based research gurus promote this and many of the teachers on my campus are doing this. Is this a violation?*

© Technically if they aren't studying the music, this is a public performance. You should have a venue license (a license to cover the building for public performances of music) from ASCAP or BMI, but neither sells such a license for K-12 schools. So you aren't legal, but you can't GET legal. The good news is that Mozart is the music most often recommended for this purpose, and his music is old enough that it is in the public domain. The bad news is that the *performance* of the music may still be covered by copyright, however. There are a few Web sites that offer free downloads of classical music recorded before performances were protected by copyright, so you might try those sites for music usable for this purpose.

Public Performance | Songs During Graduation

? *Our senior class wants to play two songs during the graduation ceremony: one when presenting their parents with roses and one the class song. The graduation will take place in the school gymnasium. Are copyright issues involved?*

© Of course there are copyright issues any time you have a public (and this is certainly public) performance of a copyrighted musical work. In the book *Copyright: The Complete Guide for Music Educators* (Music in Action, 1997), the author explains that performances such as you describe are not exempt performances. That being said, there is a Catch-22. While if such a performance were to take place at a college graduation, the college would be required to pay a blanket license for the performance of music on campus; even though the same requirement is made for K-12 schools, there is no means to pay for a K-12 blanket license. So as long as the performance of the music takes place in a school facility, you can probably get away with it. That doesn't mean that this will always be the case. With revenues for the music industry sinking rapidly, they will be looking for new revenue streams. K-12 education is a sitting duck. I predict that there will eventually be a mandatory blanket license for K-12 schools.

Public Performance | Using Background Music

? *I am training students to use a video camera, a digital camera, and video-editing software to create a daily presentation for the student body. We tape it first period and then show it to the student body at the beginning of second period. The presentation includes school announcements, book talks, student projects, etc. Would we be infringing copyright if we used a few seconds of music from CDs I own? Would that be fair use? It is face-to-face instruction.*

© The first problem is that it is NOT face-to-face instruction in the legal definition of the term. Only if a teacher is presenting curricular content in direct teaching do you have "face-to-face" instruction. An announcement-type program such as this that goes to all the students in the building is not direct teaching of curricular content since not every student is studying the same things. The second problem is that "fair use" of music can be problematic if the music is recognizable. A copyright attorney recently posted that if you can tell what the song is, you have used a "significant amount." How much is a "few seconds"? The favorable things are that you aren't charging admission, and you own the CDs. Neither is a major factor when compared to the others.

Chapter Five

Video
and Film

Video is probably the #1 copyright issue in schools. It is a double-edged sword. While students learn well from the format and it has a high interest factor, it is also the primary means of entertainment and reward, both of which are non-exempt activities as far as copyright is concerned. Reward and entertainment showings (basically any showing that is not a teacher presenting curricular content to students) are public performances, and as such require a copy of the video/film that includes public performance rights. Any copy of a video/film that has any notice on it about "home use only" does not have public performance rights.

Videos with the "home use" notation *may* be used in school as long as five requirements are met. It may be easiest to understand the five requirements if you address them as five yes/no questions. The yes/no analysis must be done on a per-performance basis. A NO answer to any of the five questions means that public performance rights are required for that performance. The five questions are:

1. Is the performance in a nonprofit educational institution?

2. Do students and teachers in a regular class give the performance?

3. Does the performance take place in a classroom or other instructional place?
4. Is the performance made from a legally acquired copy of the film/video?
5. Is the performance made in the course of direct instruction of a required curriculum topic?

Using video as rainy day recess, bus duty babysitting, perfect attendance awards, occupying time for those who are unable to take standardized tests, or rewards for those who do well on standardized tests are all types of performances that require public performance rights. Some videos may be purchased with such rights; others can be licensed on a per use or blanket basis. A school can also purchase a comprehensive license that covers public performances of films/videos of the products of a select list of producers—usually the more popular entertainment titles that would have no possibility of instructional use anyway. Purchasing such a license is a blessing and curse. The school so licensed need not worry about showing entertainment or reward videos from the producers who participate in the particular licensing program chosen. The curse appears once faculty find out they can show such videos without fear of legal repercussions. They are more likely to show entertainment videos under that scenario, therefore they may be spending more class time in non-instructional activities than a teacher without such carte blanche to employ reward and entertainment video. While not technically a copyright issue, copyright compliance seems to trigger this situation.

Generally | Archival Copies of Video

? *Our technology coordinator is purchasing a DVD burner in order to make copies of classroom/library videos. She says we are not violating copyright because we are making "an archival copy" even though we would now be using the DVD version rather than the VHS version. Is this correct?*

© Your technology coordinator is right about one thing: she is making an archival copy. The problem is that archival copies of video are not permitted under current U.S. law. The *only* medium given automatic permission for archival (backup) copies is computer software. In fact, video producers routinely SELL archival rights (not expensive, but certainly available). She would also be changing format of the materials. And the reason she is changing the format is to avoid purchasing the program in the new medium (DVD). While a transfer might be justified if the materials weren't available in digital format, any time you can purchase a DVD and you convert something from another format, you should hear all sorts of alarm bells going off.

Generally | AV Restrictions

? *Depending upon the production company, we have discovered that many videos do not fall under "fair use" even in the classroom (with the lesson plan, direct instruction, and with a legal copy of the video). We even defined what "fair use" was and they agreed that they understood, but that although the other videos that we owned would not necessarily need a license for use in the classroom when used with a lesson plan, that this company restricted the use of their videos in any setting other than personal use (at home).*

© The direct instruction piece (the five yes/no questions) is part of federal law. A company cannot just "decide" to not permit use of their materials under federal fair use exemptions. That being said, if the purchaser SIGNS A CONTRACT or buys a copy with a shrink-wrap that says "not for use in schools and libraries" you are bound by that contract. In other words, you have fair use rights UNLESS YOU CHOOSE TO GIVE THEM UP. A producer who markets educational videos but who refuses to allow the videos to be shown in instructional settings is shooting itself in the foot.

Generally | Copies for Kids

? We made a video for a centennial celebration. All the work in the video is the children's except for some images (source of images is documented with each image) and short music clips (following fair use guidelines). Parents who saw the video at the program want copies of it. Do you think this can be legally copied?

© Each child who worked on the video can have a single copy, per the multimedia guidelines.
Remember that a multimedia project MUST have a statement that it may not be copied, along with a mediagraphy citing the source of any copyright protected material used within. Those rules come from the multimedia guidelines.

Generally | *Download Data from Disc to Video*

? *Is it legal to download data from laser discs to video for classroom use? If so, can the teacher keep the video for future use?*

© No, you may never change format (laser disc to tape, record to tape) without express permission, or unless the format is obsolete. Such permission would specify how long the tape could be retained. Laser disc is rare, but not quite obsolete yet. Once laser disc players are no longer available for purchase, you would be able to transfer all your laser discs to another format of your choice IF the same content is not available for purchase in an active format.

Generally | *Editing Questionable Videos*

? *I recently found a company that will edit our videos to remove objectionable language and sexual situations. Can this be legal?*

© There are a couple of answers to this question. The company you found doesn't make a copy of your videotape—they actually snip out footage. The problem with this procedure is that video recordings are not put on tape in the same way as an audiocassette. Videotape is recorded diagonally (actually helically) on the tape, so when the tape is cut and spliced, the recorder loses its "synch." From that point on, the sound and the video will no longer be synchronized, and the mouths will not match the dialogue. If you still choose to partake of this service, be aware that copyright attorneys do not agree that this service is legal. Some contend that the doctrine of "first sale" allows a purchaser to make any use of a single copy that they choose. Others, however, find that what has been done is to create an adaptation and a derivative work. At this moment, no cases involve this particular company, but a similar company has reportedly been stopped from this practice.

A recent law, the Family Movie Act of 2005, allows videos to be encoded with tags allowing certain players to skip offensive words and scenes. The video isn't actually edited, it is just tagged so the player will know what to skip and for how long. Because the permission is statutory, these players and the videos designed to be used in them are legal for home use. The law is specifically worded to apply to home use only. Nothing in the law says anything about schools or public performances. It does NOT give permission to make expurgated copies, or to physically edit videos for content.

Generally | Film Collection for Students

? *I am hoping to create a film collection for student check out. Is it copyright infringement to buy videos and have them checked-out by students for home viewing?*

© As long as the copies you circulate are legal, and you have no prior knowledge that the videos are going to be used in an infringing manner, ("Oh, gee, thanks, Mrs. Smith! My Boy Scout Troop will love to see this on our lock-in!") you can circulate any videos you wish. A recent development has been that some videos are coming shrink-wrapped with a license visible from the outside. The license states that the videos may not be used in schools or libraries. In such a case, you may be bound by the "shrink-wrap license" and the work cannot be used. I have seen these shrink-wrapped items at places like Sam's Club and Costco.

Generally | *Loaning Videos*

? *Is there a law or a policy for buying videos from a store and using them for loan in the library like you can with books?*

© Copyright law allows the purchaser of a legitimate copy of a work to loan that work under the "first sale doctrine." However, at Sam's Clubs, Costco, and some other discount chains I have seen shrink-wrapped videos, computer software, and books that state in plain view on the wrapping "Not for sale to schools and libraries." Those items may NOT be circulated under the rulings in several U.S. Circuit Courts. You will need to determine what the rule is in your circuit to know if shrink-wrap licensing is enforceable in your circuit, but it is in most.

Generally | Mail Order Video Expurgation

? *There is a company that edits language and questionable graphic scenes from videos. They do this for videos that are sent to them, or one can order pre-edited videos. Would this be "legal" for videos used in the school setting? Also, would this change the rating from R to G? Would this violate copyright?*

© CNI_COPYRIGHT (a listserv for those who are interested in copyright matters) had a discussion about this company a while back, and the lawyers were divided on the legality. But they were pretty firm on not using those videos in a school or library setting because of the risk of exposure. The company faces the greatest risk, but if they do what I think they are doing (actually razoring out the words or cutting the tape) the synch between the sound and the image will be lost in the remainder of the tape. If they don't actually cut out the tape (making an adaptation) they must COPY your tape (an illegal copy) and then alter it. That way you would be caught with an illegal copy of the tape, and that can get YOU into trouble as well as the ones who copied it. All in all, not a good scenario.

Generally | No-Library-Loan Video

? *I am going through my elementary school video collection correcting many mistakes in labeling and inappropriate records. I found a video that has the following statement on the back of the box: "This video cassette not for resale, rental, or library loan." Should this video be in my collection? Does fair use even apply when this type of statement is on the material?*

© This is the topic of a discussion that is going on among copyright attorneys in CNI_COPYRIGHT (a listserv for those who are interested in copyright matters). Some say that this is considered a "shrink-wrap" license and is enforceable. Others say it is governed by first sale and is not enforceable. The major concern is that all book and AV publishers might decide to put these notices on their materials and libraries would not be able to circulate materials! So the short answer is: there is no answer at this point. It will likely take a court case to further define the parameters of such statements.

Generally | *Off-Air Taping*

? *A teacher has some TV broadcasts taped off-air several years ago. He has not been able to find a source from which we may purchase a copy. How do we determine that it is no longer available for purchase? And, if it is no longer available for purchase and/or broadcast is he able to use his taped version in school? I wondered if the same rule applied as with books that are no longer available for purchase, it is permissible to copy in order to use?*

© The teacher has not been able to retain those programs after 45 days post-broadcast, so the tapes are illegal for school use (personal use at home doesn't have this restriction). This isn't the same situation ("not available at a reasonable price") as replacing a book that has been damaged. This is part of the off-air taping guidelines. It may be that these tapes have NEVER been available for sale, and that is the prerogative of the copyright owner. If the program is not available for sale, and the tapes are older than 45 days past the broadcast from which they were taped, your only option will be to track down the copyright owner to request permission to use the tapes. What I'm not sure of is how you will explain how you have the tapes to begin with since under the off-air guidelines they should have been erased long ago.

Generally | Parent Videotaping Musical Performance

? *Our high school recently staged a musical, and the school's Fine Arts Department legitimately purchased the production rights for this event. A parent videotaped the performance and now would like to make copies of the videotape to sell to parents of cast members at exactly the cost of making the copies. These tapes would be used only for the enjoyment of the students' families. Will this violate copyright law? Do we need to obtain permission to copy this videotape?*

© Unless the school (or the parent) also purchased the rights to tape and distribute the production, this use would likely be a violation of copyright. The law doesn't address this specific situation, but it does address performances of music. A school may make a single copy of a musical performance, but that copy may be used only in class to critique the performance. You should seek permission to copy the tape, but you may be admitting that you have already violated the law by taping the production. I would have the school check the license it received for the production to see what rights already have been purchased. You may already have the ability to do what you propose, but that activity must be stipulated in the contract. If it isn't, you must make additional arrangements with the rights broker.

Generally | *PBS Tape Retention*

? *I've always been told to erase tapes like* Reading Rainbow *(RR) when the one-year rights expire and to re-tape them the next year. Is that still the way this works? We have some copies of RR shows that were taped a few years ago. The shows were re-aired recently. It seemed to me that if the rights were renewed for a year that we could still use the old tapes, but I've always been told the opposite. Do you know what we're really supposed to do in cases like this?*

© I'm assuming you are referring to the rights granted through your local public television station. If so, and the rights are renewed, keeping the tapes should be no problem as long as there has been no interruption in the rights. However, having tapes older than the limit without current rights would be a problem. If the tapes are used heavily, you might want to re-tape just because the used tapes will have deteriorated in quality. Tapes also degrade because of the magnetic fields of the earth, but that isn't a copyright issue!

Generally | Spontaneity and Providing Lists to Teachers

? *In your book you discuss spontaneity and write that a media specialist should not give a teacher a list of appropriate items to be copied. Does this also apply to the media specialist who provides teachers with a list/program guide to cable program listings for the month or semester? May we provide this list and ask if they desire anything to be taped off air? (The final choice would be up to the individual teacher, and the media specialist would only be advising them that the programming is available.)*

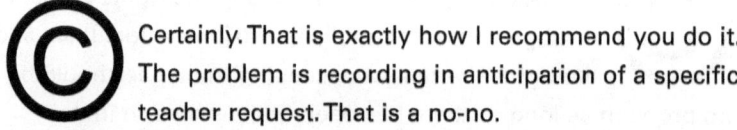 Certainly. That is exactly how I recommend you do it. The problem is recording in anticipation of a specific teacher request. That is a no-no.

Generally | Using Video Distribution Systems

? *Our fifth grade teachers want us to use our video distribution system to show a program for all the fifth-grade classes in our district. Is that a violation of copyright?*

© You can use your video distribution system to show any programs on your campus that would be permissible under the fair use exemption. The fact that the classes are seeing the program simultaneously through the video distribution system isn't a problem. However, using your distribution system to send programs beyond the campus *even if the showing would otherwise meet the fair use exemption* is not permitted. Such long-distance broadcasting always requires a license or other permission.

Generally | Video Anthology

? A teacher does an art history timeline unit each year and wants to show only 15 minutes of many different videos to introduce that segment of the timeline. She wants to dub each of these 15-minute segments onto a single cassette so she doesn't have to search for the appropriate short segment each time she teaches it. Our library owns these videos. Is this permitted?

© No, she may not legally make an anthology of the video clips under fair use. There are specific prohibitions against making anthologies. She may request permission from all of the copyright holders of the different works, and make an anthology of the ones who give permission, however. If she could limit the video segments to three minutes, and if she could put those segments into a PowerPoint presentation, she might be able to use the video under the multimedia guidelines, but she would need express permission after using the program for two years.

Generally | Video Edited for Content

? *A recent journal article said that it is all right for districts to "edit videos for content," citing the first-sale doctrine. I thought this was against copyright law? The article also stated that anyone, including libraries, could obliterate all of the foul language printed in a book and still not violate copyright law. A librarian in our district wanted to mark out some offensive language in one of his library books. I told him that the expurgation changed the author's intent, and it was against copyright. Now we are both confused.*

© It is true that you can deface the one physical copy of a book you own under first sale. When you purchase a book, you own the paper, ink, and binding that make up that copy, and you can do anything you wish with that one physical entity, from giving it away to wallpapering your study with the torn out pages. In Europe and other parts of the world, defacing an author's work may be a violation of the creator's moral rights (a form of protection for creative expression), but the creator's moral rights in the United States are much more limited. The ethical issues of censoring an author's expression will be left for another forum.

However, I will object strenuously to the ability to edit video for content. The primary problem is you can't just clip videotape (like you would edit an audiotape) to remove offensive content without completely destroying the audio synch. From the point of the initial cut, the audio would no longer match with the pictures on the screen. This problem is a result of the helical nature of video recording. So, in order to clip out offensive words or scenes, one must make a new copy of the recording, pausing to allow the offending parts to pass before continuing to record. To make the "clean" copy, you must defeat the typical copy protection installed on commercial videotapes and DVDs (a violation of the DMCA anti-circumvention provision) AND make a copy of the edited version (an illegal copy). There is currently a lawsuit pending about this very issue. A company called Clean Flicks is suing (and being sued) for doing just that! Watch the news for developments in that case.

Generally | *Video Licensing*

? *We would like to buy the video version of a television program to use in a health class. The ordering information included two different options: one for home use, and one for public performance. The company told us that we had to buy the public performance version even though the video will be used in conjunction with curriculum units. Is this enforceable by the company? There was a difference of $120 between the two different versions. My understanding of public performance is that it's for use as entertainment, rewards, fill time, babysitting, and outside of the school day usage. Am I correct?*

© You are not off base in your understanding of public performance rights, but beware of signing a license or contract that limits your fair use options. If the company doesn't sell, but instead licenses videos you are at its mercy. By signing or agreeing to a license that limits your fair use options, you only have the rights you agree to. You may not realize that you don't have to buy the video for the school. A personal video can be used as well. You might have someone buy the video personally, then reimburse that person. But watch out for that licensing issue!

In Class | After School Movie Showings

? *We have an AP history teacher who has an after-school session to show the class R-rated movies with important historical content, such as* Amistad. *Students must have parental permission and the movie coincides with the subject matter they are currently studying. It is not, however, during normal class hours. Is she violating copyright?*

© The fair use guidelines for audiovisuals don't say "no after school" but they do say the showing must include the students and teacher(s) in that class ONLY. If they let anyone in AT ALL, it is a violation. And the showing MUST occur at school.

In Class | *Making a Videotape Anthology*

? *A senior English teacher is comparing a scene in* Hamlet *from three different filmed versions. The school owns all three versions of the* Hamlet *videos, and we also subscribe to a movie licensing service. The teacher would like to transfer those three scenes to a single videotape so he doesn't have to keep switching out tapes in the VCR. Is this okay?*

© What you describe is called "making an anthology." Anthologies are not permitted in the print guidelines, which are the only copy guidelines we have, other than backup copies for computer software. There is no specific writing in the law to say that anthologies are or are not permitted in video. Your movie license has nothing to do with this because it only gives you public performance rights, which you don't need anyway since this is a curricular showing and meets all of the AV guidelines. While you might not be caught if you created and retained such a recording, I wouldn't want to have this sort of thing hanging around. If the teacher plans to do this, I would say to use as little as possible and make the copy only for the time he will use it in class, then **ERASE** and recreate it next year if he plans to use it again.

In Class | *Peripheral Movie Showings*

? *I know you can't use movies for "fun" days. However, in Personal Development we have an activity day once a week. The goal of this day is for students to find fun in drug-free activities. Each student plans an activity; sometimes this involves a movie. Is this somehow illegal?*

© Unless the content of the movie (not the activity of viewing the movie itself) is directly related to the lesson at hand, the showing is infringing. So if the student is showing how playing hopscotch is a fun non-drug activity, and the movie teaches, or contributes materially to how to play hopscotch, the showing is not infringing. Note that enrichment videos, no matter how educational they may be, are not permitted under the AV guidelines. These guidelines were designed to help teachers present content to students in regular classes. Beyond that, permission or license is required.

In Class | *Private Home Exhibition Label*

? *We have a video purchased through a standard library supplier. It's about the human body and it's obviously educational. However, there is a label on the side that says, "Company XYZ Home Video." The back of the video states, "Licensed for private home exhibition only." It seems pretty obvious from the statements that it should not be used in a school, but it was purchased from a school supplier. What can we do?*

© Educational fair use exempts you from this restriction. The producer is powerful, but they can't override federal law. What the "home use only" sticker means is that you cannot use this for a public performance. However, your educational use must be directly related to the curriculum and the lesson at hand. That means only one grade level will be watching this because you have an aligned curriculum that teaches only this aspect of the human body in this particular grade level. They must watch it while they are studying the lesson, not earlier, later, or while the PE teacher is out sick. Look back at the five tests of AV fair use as explained in the introduction to this chapter, and ask those questions about your proposed use. Any "no" responses will require public performance licensing for that showing.

In Class | Public Domain Video or Not?

? *I have a student who would like to use a video clip on Alfred Nobel in a PowerPoint presentation. What we have found so far is copyrighted. Would we be wise to ask for permission to use the ones we found?*

© I strongly suspect the material is in the public domain. Just because someone CLAIMS a copyright doesn't mean it is so. When was this video made? Nobel died in 1893. Back then publication had to be registered and renewed. Anything published before 1923 is now in the public domain. So if the video is images of Nobel, that isn't in the public domain. If the video is someone else talking about Nobel, that video would likely be protected by copyright. But the student can use 30 seconds of ANY video (even a copyright protected one) in a PowerPoint under the multimedia guidelines.

In Class | Rainy-Day Video Situations

? *We are trying to address the copyright issues with showing videos for rainy-day recess without purchasing the expensive licenses that must be renewed each year. Our district emphasizes six Pillars of Character for our students (caring, responsibility, trustworthiness). We wondered if our campus chose and announced a specific pillar to work on for the week, and it happened to be a rainy-day recess, could the kids watch a video that demonstrated that pillar in some way? Would that fall under fair use guidelines even if we didn't have public performance rights for the video?*

© You are probably going to have to answer your own question, but I will give you some additional questions to guide you. If there is a stated district curriculum (not just an "emphasis") for those pillars, and the teachers have lesson plans that incorporate the curriculum and require the use of the video to complete the lesson, then the answer might be "yes." However, if this is considered enrichment, supplemental, "general cultural value" or "educational," then the answer is "no." The fair use of video is allowed when the use is considered important to the achievement of a specific educational objective and the other four factors of AV fair use are met. Just because something might be good for students to know or something that interests students, doesn't mean that a teacher can show that work to a class. In your library video collection, you probably have (based on research I did) 50% of your videos that already come with public performance rights because the producers sell those with the videos. Check my Web page at <http://courses.unt.edu/csimpson/cright/ppr.htm> to see which of your videos has those rights. Any video with performance rights may be used in the rainy-day situations you describe. If you mark these videos with stickers, your teachers can quickly scan the video shelves for appropriate titles to use on rainy days. The videos will be of a more appropriate length, and the students might learn something substantive.

In Class | *Satellite Television*

? *Is there any way to make "fair use" out of a teacher taping a program from satellite television and using it in face-to-face instruction with her students? What if she doesn't keep it and only shows it once?*

© The off-air taping guidelines only apply to programs taped from television channels that you would be able to receive if you had an antenna. There is a slight exception made for programs broadcast simultaneously ("simulcast") over the air and sent via cable. Cable-only and satellite-delivered programmings are not covered by these off-air rules. To tape and use these types of programs, one must have permission from the copyright owner or other notification that such taping is permitted. Magazines, such as *Discovery® Channel* magazine and *Cable in the Classroom Access Learning* (formerly *Cable in the Classroom*), provide such notices. Retention of the tapes or numbers of showings has no bearing on the appropriateness of the initial taping.

In Class | Showing a Movie for a Grade-Wide Unit

? *As part of a unit on the Holocaust, the movie* Schindler's List *has been recommended for use. Would it be possible to show this video in a large-group setting, where all students in one grade level are present? All are studying this topic at the same time.*

© Yes, you can legally have this showing. The fair use guidelines say that you must have the showing in a classroom "or other instructional place." That place can be the library, the auditorium, or a similar space in the school. Just make sure that the only people attending are those enrolled in the class for which this is part of the curriculum, and make sure they see the film while they are studying the Holocaust, not before or after.

In Class | Showing Movie Clips

? *Is it a violation of copyright to show just a clip of a movie?*

© As long as the clip doesn't convey the whole message of the film, as, for instance, the final scene does in *Bonnie and Clyde*, you should be okay under fair use. Remember, you can't put that clip on another tape. You MUST run it from a full copy of the video. You might evaluate your use of the clip under the five AV use questions listed in the introduction to this chapter, as well.

In Class | Spanish Cable

? *A Spanish teacher has taped some commercials in Spanish off of a Spanish cable channel to show to her students. Is this permissible?*

© Commercials are no different from any other programming. Your problem lies in the fact that she taped off cable. If she taped the commercials from regular over-the-air channels that were being simulcast on the local cable, that is an optimum situation. The "off-air" taping rules apply. There are no "off-air" taping guidelines for cable-only programming. You will require permission from EACH copyright holder to tape and use these commercials in class. *Cable in the Classroom* magazine tracks some program-specific permissions for cable programming, but there are no blanket guidelines for cable-only programs. There are videotapes available for purchase of Spanish language commercials, as well.

In Class | *Special Education Video Reward*

? *I know that it is illegal for teachers to show videos to students as a reward (not part of the curriculum). However, in a special education class, when students reach certain personal goals, they are rewarded. In this case, would allowing a student to watch a video as a reward for completing certain goals be considered noncompliance with copyright laws?*

© Yes, such a showing would not qualify for a fair use defense. Unfortunately, copyright law doesn't make exceptions for special education or any other noncurricular showing. However, many videos in your collection probably came with public performance rights. Check my frequently changing Web page at <http://courses.unt.edu/csimpson/cright/ppr.htm> for a list of producers who include public performance rights with videos sold to schools and libraries. Videos from these companies (taking into account the few restrictions noted on the Web page) may be used in situations such as you describe.

In Class | Student Provides Video for Educational Purposes

? *If a school owns a video and the circumstances under which it is shown meet the criteria for educational purposes (actually part of a lesson plan, etc.), I know that this use complies with copyright guidelines. But what if a student brings a video from home that fits the instructional purpose of the teacher's lesson and would be appropriate to show if the school owned it? Does the situation change because the tape came from a student's house?*

© As long as the tape is purchased (not taped off-air), your use as described is fine. The law specifies only that the copy be "legally acquired," which really means that the tape isn't pirated. The tape can belong to the school, the teacher, a student, the student's parents, or a public library. The tape can even be rented. It can meet the requirements of legal acquisition even if it was taped off-air, but only if the off-air taping guidelines were followed. As an operating rule-of-thumb, you might want to restrict off-air tapes to those you make in school, so the retention and show dates can be closely tracked.

In Class | Taping Off Cable

? *What are the guidelines for the A&E® channel? A teacher wants to use some of its* Biography *programs to support her drama class—biographies of actors and actresses. Can she do this? How long can she keep the tapes? On the Web site, I didn't find any fair use guidelines for television programs or where to purchase these biographies to add to our instructional video collection.*

© A&E® is a cable/satellite-only channel. That means that the off-air permissions exemptions do not apply. There is no fair use to copy anything from a cable/satellite-only channel. However, there may be another way. Many of the cable/satellite channels give permission on a program-by-program basis to copy certain programs and retain them for varying amounts of time. You can find this information in *Access Learning* or *Satlink* magazines. *Access Learning* has an online site, <www.ciconline.com>, which lists many of the *Biography* specials. It tells you what programs can be taped, and what retention rights are available. Some programs also provide supplementary teaching materials.

In Class | Teacher Owned Disney Films

? *My principal brought a teacher-owned copy of the Disney film,* Pocahontas, *and wants it shown on the media distribution system to grades 6-7 just before the Thanksgiving holiday dismissal. The teachers involved have a complete lesson plan with objectives. Is this legal?*

© As long as there is a lesson plan with a direct connection to the video, this is a legal showing. I assume the Jamestown settlement is part of the district curriculum for these grade levels.

Now, pedagogically this is an indefensible act. The Disney *Pocahontas* video has been shown to be historically and culturally inaccurate. A learning theory known as Media Richness Theory infers that three years from now the students will remember the vivid impression made by the erroneous video and not the study of the real facts. A better teaching/learning scenario would be to show a SCENE from the video, and have the students divide into groups to research all the errors found in the scene. Some might research the clothing, others the historical facts, or food, or shelter, or other aspects of the life of the Native Americans or colonists. This would be an appropriate use of media, and would provide an information literacy tie-in as well.

In Class | Videotaped Booktalks

? *I would like to create a few videotaped booktalks (mostly for use with classes that can't make it to the library media center but can watch videos in the classroom). To do this, I would feature between five and seven books for 3–5 minutes. Each book would be discussed (genre, plot, characters) and shown on the videotape. Do I need to get permission from the publishers/authors to hold up and discuss a book on videotape?*

© You don't need to worry. Your booktalks (if written down) are your own copyright. You may even do *short* excerpts from the books since that would fall under fair use as "criticism." I'm assuming that you will use these for your own school rather than marketing them. That situation would involve an entirely different analysis.

Public Performance | Broadcasting a Video

? *Our broadcasting system is up and running here at my school and teachers have been told that they cannot broadcast videos rented from any video store. They were also told no broadcasting of videos individual teachers have purchased for their own home use. That doesn't sound right.*

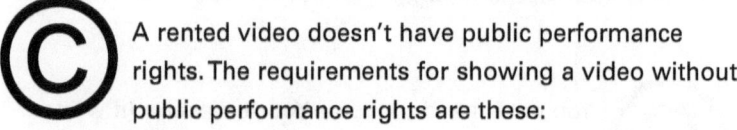 A rented video doesn't have public performance rights. The requirements for showing a video without public performance rights are these:

1. Nonprofit educational institution,

2. Shown by teachers and students in a regularly scheduled class,

3. Shown in a classroom or other instructional place,

4. Shown from a legally acquired copy of the program (the rental store bought it, so it is legal), and

5. Showing is a material part of direct teaching on a curricular topic.

Now, before we go on, we need to address the issue of "broadcasting." I assume that this is a media distribution system, not true broadcast. A media distribution system does not leave your campus. If you are sending this programming off campus, all educational exemptions are out the window and you must purchase (very expensive) broadcast rights. If the distributions stay within your own campus, you can rely on the regular educational exemptions.

You may use a "home use only" video from ANY legal source as long as you meet the five exemptions above. If you don't (using a video for reward, for example), you need public performance rights.

Chapter Five: Video and Film

Public Performance | *Charging Movie Admission Fees*

? *A teacher has decided to show a movie for entertainment purposes on the school premises. He told the principal that he has acquired the performance rights to show the movie. He is going to charge students a $2 admission. Does the right to show a movie also include the right to charge admission and profit from it? The money would be used in some way for the students.*

© Public performance rights permit a showing to a group outside a family and its immediate circle of friends in situations that don't qualify for the educational exemption. However, they don't usually convey the right to charge admission. For the right to charge admission, an additional license or contract is required. There are brokers who will license or contract for-profit showings, also called nontheatrical showings. Note that "for profit" doesn't necessarily mean that you are going to make more money than you spend, only that you are going to collect admission fees.

Public Performance | Licensing for DVDs and Videos

? *I only use DVDs and videos for instruction, so if I understand correctly, I can purchase them from anywhere for instructional use. If my PTA decided that they wanted to show one during recess, could they purchase a public performance license and show these same DVDs and videos?*

© Yes, no, and maybe. You can purchase them "from anywhere" for educational use UNLESS they have a shrink-wrap license that says they are not for schools or libraries. I see those frequently at Sam's Club and Costco. If they want to show the videos at recess AND THE PRODUCER IS ONE OF THE ONES COVERED BY THE LICENSE, you can show them for reward or entertainment purposes. Remember that license only covers about 20 of the most popular entertainment producers like Disney, Warner Bros., etc. Verify first.

Public Performance | Number of Program Showings Allowed

? *May a program taped off the air be shown twice in 10 days? For example, if a teacher has four sections of a class, can he show it to only two of them? Must he show it to those four sections as part of the same lesson, or may it be divided?*

© Under the fair use exemption, a program taped off the air may be shown twice in a 10-day period. If the tape cannot be shown in a single class period, the showings may certainly be divided. As long as each class sees the entire program no more than twice in the 10-day period, you should be okay. All four sections may see the taping.

Public Performance | *Private Showings in Movie Theaters*

? *The local theater has agreed to do a private showing of a video to students (50-100) who have earned the right by participating in a summer reading incentive program. The participating school must provide the video/DVD. Is it possible to become involved in this type of activity without violating copyright laws? If so, how?*

© I don't see how this type of showing could be within fair use. It's your video; you are just getting the hall for free. You will have students and teachers who are NOT part of a regularly scheduled class. You are showing the entire video. It isn't face-to-face instruction, and it isn't in a classroom or other instructional place, though the later might be marginal. It doesn't meet ANY of the AV guidelines. Now, if this theater has some blanket license for the producer of the film you are planning to show (which you would want to verify), you MIGHT be okay.

Public Performance | Showing Movies on Busses

? *Our school will charter large, commercial busses for an extended trip. The busses have VCRs and TVs. We would like to show a tape of a movie owned by one of the teachers to keep the children occupied while we make this lengthy trip. Is this legal?*

© Probably not unless performance rights were acquired with the tape. In order for a videotape performance to be considered fair use, all of the following must apply:

1. The performance must take place in a classroom or other instructional place,

2. The performance must be conducted by students or teachers,

3. The performance must be in the course of face-to-face teaching activities, and

4. The performance must be made with a legally acquired copy of the work.

This use of video is not "face-to-face" instruction. It probably involves some people who are not students and teachers in the class, such as a bus driver or chaperones, and the bus might be considered a bit strange for an instructional locale. The copyright holder, however, could grant (or sell) you one-time public performance rights. Contact them directly. The company that sells public performance licenses to schools sometimes includes "bus rights" with that license, so you will want to check your license agreement if you have purchased one of those.

Public Performance | Showing Videos to the Entire School

? We have several videos that the administration shows to our entire school to tie in with our character standards, which are now included as part of our state and regional accreditation curriculum. The teachers focus on such traits as respect and responsibility for a period of time and want every curriculum area to focus on that trait at the same time. Is it permissible to show a video purchased by the school to the entire student body when it ties into a school-wide theme or curriculum unit, or do public performance rights apply here?

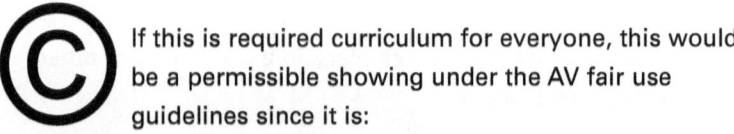 If this is required curriculum for everyone, this would be a permissible showing under the AV fair use guidelines since it is:

1. In a nonprofit educational institution,
2. The performance is by and for students and teachers in the class,
3. The performance takes place in the classroom or other instructional place,
4. The copy is legally acquired, and
5. The performance is directly related to the lesson and the curriculum.

The only possible problem is that the showing is dictated by the administration rather than by the classroom teacher (a "top-down" versus a "bottom-up" model). As long as a teacher could opt out of the showing, or all teachers agree to the showing, this proposal would meet all the necessary requirements.

Public Performance | Synch Rights with Video

? *Our senior class has a company put together a slide show set to popular music that is shown at graduation each year. The company does charge the school for the one copy. The senior class advisers have raised some questions. Does this violate any music rights? Secondly, this year the advisors would like to be able to give each senior a CD copy of the slide show at no charge. Do we need to check with the company who made the video to see if we have the right to give away copies?*

© What is your contract with the company? Has the company cleared the rights to the music? Just putting the music on the CD as accompaniment requires a synch license, plus duplication rights if you are making copies. You will need to pay those rights for all the copies you are going to make. You probably also need clearance for both the video AND the recognizable images of individuals.

Public Performance | Taping Episodes of a PBS Series

? *If a teacher completes a request form to videotape a program, does it need to be for one precise episode of a program, or may they request that you tape the program every day of the school year? A teacher has requested that I tape all episodes of a series from PBS. The programs have a three-year retention right for educational usage, and the teacher does not know what the different episodes are about but has requested them for use in her science class at a future time.*

© Unless the retention rights allow public performances, the request should be episode-specific. You may not show programs just because they are educational. They absolutely must relate to the specific curriculum at hand. Taping in anticipation of use is not permitted. Check with your local PBS station for rights pertaining to a particular series.

Public Performance | Video PPR

? *I recently saw some DVDs at a great price in a local store. I didn't buy them because I wasn't sure about their licensing. Do the DVDs that I've purchased through vendors have the public performance licensing and the ones in the bookstores just have home viewing? Is there a way to tell on the cover?*

© If you are getting public performance rights, you generally know it. A video bought at a consumer outlet is virtually assured to be home use only (but can be used instructionally because public performance rights are not required if the AV guidelines are met.) Some videos purchased from some educational producers come with PPR when they are sold to schools directly (not necessarily through jobbers). See my Web page at <http://courses.unt.edu/csimpson/cright/ ppr.htm> for a current list.

Chapter Six

Multimedia, Software, and Distance Learning

Multimedia, once the bane of a teacher's existence because of the complex copyright issues involved, has become simple to administer because of the multimedia guidelines. As long as the user knows a few pieces of information, correct usage is easy to determine. For a proper evaluation you need to know these things:

1. Is this a school use?
2. Who will be using the material?
3. What material will be used?
4. How much of the material will be used (in seconds, pages, minutes, images, etc.)?
5. Where will the material be kept?
6. How long will the material be kept?
7. How many copies are needed?

Educators and producers wrote the multimedia guidelines, so they are clearly written and easy to understand. See *Copyright for Schools: A Practical Guide, 4th Edition* (Linworth Publishing, Inc., 2005), or any comprehensive copyright reference work for complete information about the multimedia guidelines.

Computer software is actually one of the simpler media as far as copyright is concerned. Governed primarily by license, about the only thing that is odd for computer software is that one may make an archival or backup copy of disks or CDs for use in case the original is lost or damaged. That permission applies to no other forms of media.

Distance learning, and to some degree Web distribution of materials by schools, is governed by the TEACH Act. Passed in 2002, TEACH has finally given mostly clear guidelines on using copyright protected materials in distance learning situations. Distance learning can also encompass Web support of face-to-face teaching, as well. Since there are no specific fair use rules for Internet materials, TEACH went a long way toward setting some boundaries for using these materials. Since the TEACH Act is very complex and involves three groups of school professionals, consult *Copyright for Schools: A Practical Guide, 4th Edition* (Linworth Publishing, Inc., 2005), or any comprehensive copyright guide for complete details.

Generally | AR AWOL

? *About four years ago, my school system purchased a basal reader that had Accelerated Reader™ (AR) tests for each story. The AR disk was lost or misplaced for the 4th grade book. I want to borrow the 4th grade disk from another school in our district, but we are uncertain of copyright regulations. If I borrow the AR disk from another school, would I be violating copyright laws?*

© If you purchased the original 4th grade disk and didn't make a backup copy of it (shame on you for missing that opportunity—make one of the others ASAP) you can get a copy from another school and make TWO copies—one to use and one to put away "just in case." You can do this because the CD is computer software, and copyright law allows a backup or archival copy of computer software.

Generally | *Burning CDs*

? *One of our school libraries wants to check out data CDs to students to take home. They purchased a CD burner with the idea of making a copy for checkout while keeping the original as an archive. My "gut" feeling is that you can't make an archival video and check out copies, so it is probably not legal to do the same with a CD (unless the license specifically states that you can copy for checkout).*

© The only medium for which backup copies are legal is computer software, so it is okay to make a backup of a CD-ROM, but not okay to make a backup of a DVD movie or an audio CD. You want to make sure that you make only one backup copy and circulate only one while protecting the other. The software should not also be installed on any machines at the school or library. The thing to remember is that if you know (or suspect) that the borrower plans to make illegal copies of the CD, you should refuse to loan the software. The software should also go with a copyright notice that states that the work is protected by copyright. See *Copyright for Schools: A Practical Guide, 4th Edition* (Linworth Publishing, Inc., 2005), or any comprehensive copyright reference for the required text of the notice.

Generally | Discontinued Software

? *We use a wonderful software program that's easy for middle school students and teachers to use, but it's been discontinued. Because we can no longer get additional site licenses, though we'd be willing to pay for them, may we make copies from what we have? As newer and more machines are added to the district, we're caught in a bind. So far we've found nothing we really like as well as the old program.*

© You can keep installing the software on replaced computers (one computer dies and you install that license on a replacement machine), but you can't make copies of the software for new or additional machines. You might work out something with the producer to keep using it, or get permission from them, but without that permission you're committing piracy. Piracy results in major fines. Remember, out-of-print does not equal out of copyright!

Generally | Donated Software

? *A teacher wants to donate computer software to our school. However, it has been opened. Can she donate it with a letter stating that fact for our files?*

© This should be no problem as long as she removes it from her hard drive first. Just get her to send a letter stating she is donating it to the school and has retained no copies. That should cover your bases.

Generally | *Fair Use on the Web?*

? *For summer reading, our history teacher would like to assign an essay from a collection. I've purchased one copy of the (expensive) book and discovered that the essay in question is 38 pages long. As a way to conserve paper I suggested that maybe it could be uploaded onto a secure Web page that the students would access by using a password. We hope that this use is fair use.*

© One essay (if less than 2,500 words) may be copied in multiple copies for classroom use (the summer reading issue is a bit dicey, especially if is a voluntary program, not a regular class) one time with short notice without permission. The problem here is the length of this essay. It's clearly out of bounds of the print guidelines. You're going to need to clear this, either with the publisher or through the Copyright Clearance Center. CCC can do it quickly, but it will cost you money. The publisher may be slow, but may give you the rights for free. Another option is to put the book on reserve at the public library. The students may then decide to make their own copies for convenience, but the teacher may not require the students to make copies of the essay.

Putting the essay on the Web is a change of format and wide distribution. The TEACH Act allows you to put audiovisual works in "reasonable and limited portions" online, but textbooks and readings are excluded, as are workbooks. Of course, if you can get permission from the copyright holder, you can do whatever they give you permission to do.

Generally | Installing Computer Software

? *When installing computer software, is installation of each piece permitted on only one machine at a time unless we have a site license?*

© Read the license that comes with each piece of software. The type may be small, but the impact is large. Most software licenses say that you may install the software on only one machine at a time. That means you can put the software on computer A, use it, and then remove it before installing it on computer B. Some programs on CD-ROM will not work unless the CD is in the drive, but they also install some software to the computer's hard disk to make the program run faster since hard disks are faster than CD-ROM drives. Since the program won't run without the CD in the drive, some people like to install the hard disk portion to multiple computers so that any computer is ready to run the CD if it is available. This is problematic if the software license says it may be installed on only one computer at a time.

Generally | *Installing Single-User CDs*

? *Is it legal to install a single-user CD on more than one computer? I'm thinking it should be okay because you must have the CD to use the program, so you couldn't have multiple people using the same CD.*

© You must read your license to know for sure. Unless it specifically says "multiple loading" is permitted, then no, you may not legally do this. The reason is that the copyright police will come in with a program that tallies installations of software. If you have, for example, one Grolier's CD, but you install it on six computers, so you can pop the CD into whichever machine is vacant, the tally program will show six installs of Grolier's, and you will be liable for five violations.

Generally | *Installing Software on Circulating Computers*

? *I have a CD-ROM that I would like to circulate with any of my computers. Can I install the CD onto all the machines since it will only be able to run with the CD in the drive?*

© Unfortunately, no. Unless your software license (the one with the tiny print) gives information to the contrary, you may only install the software (ANY part of the software) on one machine at a time. That means that if the CD requires a portion to be loaded on to the hard disk of the computer, that portion may only be loaded on one machine at a time. CDs that don't require any hard disk installation may have icons created on multiple machines since the icons aren't part of the computer program.

Generally | Lab Pack License

? *We ordered a lab pack computer program. The license explains that it "grants you a nonexclusive license for up to five users at a single location." May these five licenses be split between teachers, or is a "single location" one classroom? The lab pack also gives permission to make six copies of the User's Manual/Teacher's Guide (which makes me think we might be able to split the license among classrooms).*

© Barring any other language in the license that restricts your installation to a single room, you should be able to install the five copies on any machines in your building. Just verify that no more than five installations are made and you are good to go. Remember, this is *no more than five installations*, not five copies in use at once. There is a big difference between those choices!

Generally | Linking Internet Sites

? *Do we require permission to link an Internet site to our school's Web page or is it simply a courtesy to obtain permission before doing so?*

© There isn't a law that says you must get permission, but there are several court cases dealing with that problem. One involves Microsoft linking to the Ticketmaster site. Ticketmaster claimed that Microsoft profited from having the Ticketmaster link on the MS Web page. Ticketmaster never gave permission for the link. There are also many suits involving links to certain comics' characters' pages. If they find you have linked to them, they'll jump on you fast. So make up your own mind about the risk, but it's always safer to ask. Many educational Web sites invite links.

Generally | Linking Web Sites

? *Do we need to write for permission to put a Web page link to ABC News or other commercial Web sites when listing possible resources (links) from our home page?*

© Well, the answer is, "It depends." A simple link should be okay, but it is good netiquette to ask or tell the site that you are linking so they know to expect more traffic or so they can decline to affiliate with your organization (it sometimes happens).

The problem comes in when you use frames. On a frames page, the link looks like it is your own page (the URL at the top never changes from your page URL), so the other site might complain that you are "stealing" or misrepresenting their content to display it under your name. So the short answer is, better ask permission. You may not need it, but if you have it, you are home free.

Generally | *Partial CD Installation Permission*

? *You wrote that CD-ROM programs may not be partially installed on more than one computer even though the CD must be in the computer for actual usage. Would this be acceptable if the users of the CD-ROM programs to be used in this manner received permission from the producer/publisher of the CD?*

© The conditions I describe are those allowed under fair use with no permission. If you get permission or a license that gives greater rights, goferit! In that case, however, you are limited to what the license will (or will not) allow.

Generally | URL Bookmarks

? *Is it legal to bookmark sites in anticipation of future research a teacher might want to use?*

© No problem with bookmarks. Lists of URLs are just facts, and they aren't copyrightable, in and of themselves. Of course, if you bookmark them too far in advance the URLs may change, but that isn't a copyright issue!

Multimedia | *Background Music*

? *To use a compact disc for background music in a multimedia presentation, I hook the CD player directly to the computer so I don't have to make an actual copy of the recording. Is that copyright infringement?*

© If you use it once, for class presentation, you are okay. It's the amount and frequency that causes problems. Of course, a student can use just about anything for schoolwork. Teachers don't have the same latitude.

Multimedia | *Borrowing Theme Music from Video*

? *If we are doing an original PowerPoint presentation for a class project, can we borrow the theme music from a popular movie if we give credit to the artists? We are not going to enter this project in competition or publish this creative work.*

© Because this is a multimedia production within the definition of the multimedia copyright guidelines, you are bound by those guidelines. Just giving credit isn't sufficient. As an analogy, suppose you wanted to "borrow" the entire text of a popular novel, but you credit the author. Do you think you might be in trouble for doing that? Certainly! The same holds true with music. Under fair use you may use a short portion of the original work under a claim of fair use. In the case of copyright-protected music in a multimedia production, you will be limited to a 10% or maximum 30 seconds excerpt from the original music, but the time need not be continuous. The guidelines are short and easy to read. Find the original text at: <http://www.utsystem.edu/OGC/IntellectualProperty/ccmcguid.htm>.

Multimedia | Electronic Portfolio and Copyright Permissions

? *I have an electronic portfolio. Currently I have it on my personal Web site. I've e-mailed state legislators regarding pending bills for school and library funding. I've received both e-mail and written letters from them. Would I need permission from the individuals to include the text of my e-mail to the legislators and their replies in my portfolio?*

© A lot depends on who wrote the e-mails. Generally, e-mails are the intellectual property of the person who wrote them. The recipient owns the copy that he received, but does not have the right to redistribute that copy. However, if a federal government employee within the scope of his duty wrote the e-mail, there is no copyright by law. Those e-mails you can distribute (via the Web) as you wish. If state government employees send the e-mails, you will need to check with your state to see if they claim copyright in the works of employees (as this would be work for hire).

Multimedia | Looping

? *If I download 10% or 30 seconds of an audio to insert into Movie Maker, can I use that same 30 seconds as a loop, over and over throughout the project?*

© Under the multimedia guidelines you can use 30 seconds of audio (or 10% whichever is less) in a multimedia presentation. The source of the audio must be a legal one, so use caution in your downloads. The guidelines don't say how many times you can use the clip in a given presentation, so I would assume a loop is not prohibited.

Multimedia | *Movie Clips in PowerPoint*

? *A teacher is making a PowerPoint presentation for a group of chemistry teachers and students. He wants to insert clips from movies. I thought this was a change of format and not allowed, but it is educational and the clips are short. Does the change in format override the fair use policy? Could he show the clips directly from a DVD (one at a time) if they are not embedded in the presentation?*

© Check the multimedia guidelines for the rules regarding using video in a presentation. He can use up to three minutes or 10% (whichever is less) of a movie in a PowerPoint presentation as long as all the requirements are met. You can find the guidelines at <www.utsystem.edu/OGC/IntellectualProperty/ccmcguid.htm>.

Multimedia | *Scanning Worksheets*

? *I am building a Web page for an algebra II course. Can I scan a worksheet from my teacher's edition to use as an assignment for my students? My site is password protected.*

© If the sheet is within a PowerPoint presentation, the multimedia fair use guidelines say you can do this, but only for two weeks, unless the file can be protected from copying (not possible through most browsers at this time). Beyond that time you must have permission. There are other requirements such as a notice on the site that there are copyrighted materials. See the multimedia fair use guidelines at <www.utsystem.edu/OGC/IntellectualProperty/ccmcguid.htm> for more detailed information.

The TEACH Act says that workbooks, worksheets, and other consumable materials cannot be mounted on course Web sites, even when password protected.

Multimedia | Showing Student-Made Multimedia Products

? *We want to have a technology fair to show off the multimedia products our students have made using our new technology. What copyright implications do we need to consider?*

© Students and teachers in a classroom have nearly *carte blanche* when it comes to performing with or displaying the products they make for class work. However, performances or displays to groups outside the class can become non-protected public performances. If the products or displays contain material wholly made by the students and teachers, there is no problem whatsoever in performing or displaying the works for any audience, provided the creator gives permission. Problems creep in when creators have incorporated music, art, or video clips from copyrighted items into their class projects.

Students are entitled, under the fair use exemption, to use brief parts of copyrighted works in their class work as long as the only persons viewing the materials are students and teachers of that class. That restriction could be extended to the parents of the students at an open house. A public display to persons who don't qualify—such as anyone who happens to drop in at the technology fair—would likely be a public performance or display not protected under the educational fair use exemption. Naturally, every person has the ability to claim fair use in using portions of copyright protected works. For a public performance such as you mention a standard four-part fair use analysis would be in order.

Multimedia | *Student Multimedia in Staff Development*

? *If you take a student-produced multimedia work to a staff development session where it is presented to other teachers, and it is well within the two-year period of its being produced, and all the length, citation, etc. requirements of the multimedia guidelines are met, what else do the teachers need to do to show and discuss the student work?*

© The problem here is twofold: The student owns the copyright in his own work. The multimedia guidelines let him use the project indefinitely as long as the use is personal. Since the student isn't doing this presentation, this use isn't personal. So the teacher is going to need to get permission from the STUDENT (actually most likely the student's parents) to use the portions of the work that the student created. Then there comes the issue of the copyrighted portions that the student "borrowed" for the presentation. Since we have left the safe harbor of the multimedia guidelines, we must fall back on a fair use analysis of the borrowed portions. You are going to have to do the four-factor "weighing" test on each piece of copyrighted work contained therein. If they pass, then the teachers can likely use the production in the workshop.

Multimedia | *Using Music in PowerPoint*

? *The principal in my school would like to use a popular "top-40" type song along with a PowerPoint presentation. If the audio is played to coincide with the presentation, not taped onto the computer, nor modified in any way, do we need special permission?*

© Basically, your principal can use up to 30 seconds of the song without permission. He may retain the presentation for two years from the date of its first use. He MUST have, as the first slide in his presentation, the statement, "This presentation contains copyrighted material used under the educational fair use exemption to U.S. Copyright law" (or words to that effect). The last slide(s) of the program must include a mediagraphy that includes the copyright information (copyright date and copyright holder) for each piece of copyrighted material used in the presentation.

Multimedia | Workshop Use of a Student Multimedia Project

? *Can I take a student's multimedia project to a teacher's workshop outside the school district to use as an example if I obtain the student's and parent's permission?*

© If the student did all the work on the project—there is no copyrighted material included in the project that the student did not create—then permission of the student and parent is all that is required. If, however, the project includes copyrighted material used by the student under the multimedia fair use guidelines, only the student may use the project for workshops. The teacher may not retain copies of the work for any reason.

Distance Learning | *Rules for Video Use in Distance Learning*

? *The last part of your answer in reference to showing videos said, "However, using your distribution system to send programs beyond the campus, even if the showing otherwise meets the fair use exemption, is not permitted." This is a concern because we have a distance learning class originating from our site, and the teacher at times has used video. What rules apply to video use in a distance learning environment?*

© Good question. The TEACH Act addresses the use of video in distance learning classes. The law allows dramatic and audiovisual works to be used in "reasonable and limited portions" and in amounts typical of a class session. That explanation is confusing because in a class session a teacher could use an entire video, yet the law specifically states that distance learning use must be "limited." Until there is a court case to give us more definition, we are divided between complete and limited.

Chapter Seven

Management of Copyright

Managing copyright takes the patience of Job and the wisdom of Solomon. Walking the fine line between obeying the law and meeting the needs of students and teachers can be nearly impossible. Nevertheless, administrators, technicians, librarians, and teachers must present an honest front for highly observant students who will mimic what they see.

The key to managing copyright is consistency: the same expectations of students and teachers for compliance. Schools where copyright compliance is expected have someone on staff who has a thorough knowledge of copyright and its nuances. That person can manage the complex politics of maintaining compliance while simultaneously keeping one's collegial relationships in working order. The job requires honesty, astute observation, and a combination of curiosity and distrust. But the process is grounded upon policies and rules.

Policies | Copyright Policy

? *Our school administration is reconsidering our copyright policy to include electronic formats and Web sites. What should we include?*

© If your current policy is a good one, it will not need updating. The policy shouldn't be medium-specific. It should state that employees will follow the current federal law, and it should outline the consequences for disobeying. If your policy is appropriately written, changes in the law will be covered automatically. However, you will need to train your staff on changes in the law and on the impact of copyright on new technologies.

Policies | *Finding a Copyright Attorney*

? *If I don't trust my own judgment on a particularly sticky copyright issue, how can I find an attorney who specializes in that field?*

© Your school district's attorney may be well versed in legal matters unique to schools, such as Title 9 and state education mandates. Unfortunately he or she is seldom an expert in copyright as well. As you know from another specialized field, medicine, when things get complicated you want a specialist. Ask for recommendations from other attorneys, or call the local bar association. If all else fails, look in the yellow pages for attorneys certified in copyright, trademarks, and patents. Certification is your assurance that the attorney has taken extra training and has passed rigorous exams in the field. Also, most attorneys will give you an hour of consultation for a modest fee—usually in the neighborhood of $200-300. For really complicated problems, this expert opinion will give you the confidence to stick to your guns or will allow you to back down gracefully.

Documentation | *Photocopier Warning Notice*

? *In your book you have included the warning notice concerning copyright restrictions (Title 17, United States Code). This notice covers use of photocopies very well but does not seem to cover usage of videos and VCR equipment. Is there any official notice you would recommend that I could place on all VCRs owned by the media center to protect my liability as the librarian?*

© I recommend you affix the notice that typically goes on photocopiers [Warning: Some materials may be protected by copyright (Title 17, U.S.C.). The user is responsible for any infringement.] This sticker is generally sufficient to protect the library in cases of unattended copying. Of course, if you are helping or watching, all bets are off.

Documentation | *Site License Definition*

? *Could you please clarify the definition of "site" in the term "site license"? This issue primarily refers to schools that have more than one campus—let's say a lower school and an upper school. Does the site license apply to both campuses? I'm under the impression that each campus, although technically part of the same school, is considered a separate site.*

© The definition of site is going to depend on the contract with the software company. If your school does not have traditional grade designations, you would want to clarify that issue with the company before you issue the purchase order. A license is a contract, so it is entirely at the discretion of the agreeing parties. If you purchase the license under the name of the entire school, not as the "lower school" or "upper school," the license would likely cover the entire campus, but that is something only lawyers can decide absent specific language in the contract.

Chapter Eight

Permissions Issues

An old saying says that it is better to beg forgiveness than to ask permission. In the case of copyright infringement, it's just the opposite. Begging forgiveness generally means the involvement of lawyers and fines; but getting permission can be a long and sometimes frustrating process. At the same time, some permissions are exceedingly simple. The key to permission issues is sufficient time to receive a response. When the proposed use is too close in time to expect a reply to a permission request, fair use rules kick in. But knowing when and how to request permission is key to legal use of materials in schools.

Central Reproduction

? *My school purchased several sets of materials with the following instructions:*

"Reproduction of materials for use by an individual teacher in his/her classroom and not for commercial sale is permissible. Reproduction of these materials for an entire grade level, school, or school system is strictly prohibited."

Could this mean that it is permissible to put the materials in a central location for each grade level and allow each teacher to copy the particular pages that the teacher wishes to use with their individual class? Or, is it necessary to purchase a set for each teacher?

© In my interpretation, you can put a set in the central location and each teacher can make copies for his or her own class. Be careful, though, that teaching teams or grade levels don't start making copies en masse. That is not permitted by this license or by fair use.

Publisher Permission

? *I need to get permission to use some copyrighted materials. I've been told that if I submit three requests for such permission, and hear nothing back, that by default, permission is granted (provided I keep a record of those three requests). Have you heard of this?*

© It would be great for us if that were true, but unfortunately copyright owners are not required to respond to requests for permission. Unless you get an affirmative response, you cannot use the material.

www.ingramcontent.com/pod-product-compliance
Lightning Source LLC
Chambersburg PA
CBHW031552300426
44111CB00006BA/277